How To Read Music

WISE PUBLICATIONS
part of The Music Sales Group

London / New York / Paris / Sydney / Copenhagen / Berlin / Madrid / Tokyo

Published by
Wise Publications
14-15 Berners Street, London W1T 3LJ, UK.

Exclusive Distributors:
Music Sales Limited
Distribution Centre, Newmarket Road,
Bury St Edmunds, Suffolk IP33 3YB, UK.
Music Sales Corporation
257 Park Avenue South, New York, NY 10010,
United States of America.
Music Sales Pty Limited
120 Rothschild Avenue, Rosebery, NSW 2018, Australia.

Order No. AM986887
ISBN: 978-1-84609-727-0
This book © Copyright 2007 Wise Publications,
a division of Music Sales Limited.

Text by James Sleigh.
Music examples by Mike Sheppard.
Audio examples arranged and recorded by Mike Sheppard.
Book layout and design by Artemis Music Limited.
(www.artemismusic.com)
Edited by Ann Farmer & Chris Harvey.
Cover design by Michael Bell Design.
Cover image courtesy of Martin Barraud/Stone/Getty Images.
Printed in the EU.

Your Guarantee of Quality
As publishers, we strive to produce every book to the highest commercial standards.
The music has been freshly engraved and the book has been carefully designed to
minimise awkward page turns and to make playing from it a real pleasure.
Particular care has been given to specifying acid-free, neutral-sized paper made from
pulps which have not been elemental chlorine bleached.
This pulp is from farmed sustainable forests and was produced with special regard for the environment.
Throughout, the printing and binding have been planned to ensure a sturdy,
attractive publication which should give years of enjoyment.
If your copy fails to meet our high standards, please inform us and we will gladly replace it.

www.musicsales.com

Contents

Introduction											9

Chapter 1:		The Basics						13
	Pitch										14
	Rhythm										15
	Naming the notes							19
	Introducing the octave						20
	The basics of rhythm						22
	Bars and beats on the stave					23

Chapter 2:		Rhythm							25
	Note values									26
	The minim									28
	The crotchet								30
	The quaver									32
	The semiquaver								34

Chapter 3:		Sound & Silence					37
	The semibreve rest							38
	The minim rest								39
	The crotchet rest							40
	The quaver rest								41
	The semiquaver rest							42

Chapter 4:		Accidentals						45
	Tones and semitones							49
	Flats in practice							53
	Sharps, flats – and naturals				56

Chapter 5:		Put It Together					59
	Rhythm workout								60
	Pitch workout								62
	Real life examples							64
	Listening examples							66
	Hints and tips for learning					68

Chapter 6:		Dots & Ties						71
	Introducing the dot							73
	Ties and barlines							75
	Syncopation									77
	The push									80

Contents

Chapter 7:   **Time & Key**   **83**

Waltz time   84

Measuring the beat   86

Different time signatures   88

Back to accidentals   90

What do key signatures mean?   92

Chapter 8:   **Navigation**   **95**

Different endings   97

Back to the beginning   98

The Coda   100

Chapter 9:   **The Bass Clef**   **103**

The bass clef and ledger lines   107

Chapter 10:   **Keys & Scales**   **109**

The major scale   109

Tones and semitones   111

Chapter 11:   **Intervals**   **115**

Beyond the octave   119

Chapter 12:   **Compound Time**   **121**

From six to 12   123

The pick-up bar   125

Chapter 13:   **Articulation**   **127**

Dynamics   127

Articulating individual notes   130

Tempo   133

Ornamentation   135

Chapter 14:   **Three Into Two**   **139**

Taking tuplets further   141

Triplets and compound meters   142

Chapter 15:   **Harmony**   **145**

Triads   145

The harmonised scale   150

Inversions   151

The Roman Numeral system   154

Taking harmonisation further   156

Worksheet answers   **160**

Index   **173**

Audio examples

Chapter 1: The Basics
Audio track 1   20
Audio track 2   22
Audio track 3   22

Chapter 2: Rhythm
Audio track 4   25
Audio track 5   27
Audio track 6   28
Audio track 7   30
Audio track 8   32
Audio track 9   34

Chapter 3: Sound & Silence
Audio track 10   38
Audio track 11   39
Audio track 12   40
Audio track 13   41
Audio track 14   43
Audio track 15   43
Audio track 16   43

Chapter 4: Accidentals
Audio track 17   48
Audio track 18   53
Audio track 19   57

Chapter 5: Put It Together
Audio track 20   61
Audio track 21   63
Audio track 22   64
Audio track 23   64
Audio track 24   64
Audio track 25   65
Audio track 26   65
Audio track 27   66

Audio track 28   66
Audio track 29   66
Audio track 30   67
Audio track 31   67
Audio track 32   67

Chapter 6: Dots & Ties
Audio track 33   74
Audio track 34   76
Audio track 35   76
Audio track 36   78
Audio track 37   78
Audio track 38   79
Audio track 39   79
Audio track 40   81
Audio track 41   81

Chapter 7: Time & Key
Audio track 42   84
Audio track 43   84
Audio track 44   85

Chapter 8: Navigation
Audio track 45   96
Audio track 46   96
Audio track 47   97
Audio track 48   97
Audio track 49   98
Audio track 50   99
Audio track 51   100

Chapter 10: Keys & Scales
Audio track 52   109
Audio track 53   112

Audio examples

All the audio examples referred to in this book can be found at **www.hybrid publications.com**

Look out for the audio track logo (see below). Every time you see it, check out the website for audio clips that will demonstrate the music examples.

Audio track

Chapter 11: Intervals

Audio track 54   116

Chapter 12: Compound Time

Audio track 55   121
Audio track 56   121
Audio track 57   122
Audio track 58   122
Audio track 59   123
Audio track 60   123

Chapter 13: Articulation

Audio track 61   128
Audio track 62   130
Audio track 63   131
Audio track 64   133
Audio track 65   134
Audio track 66   134
Audio track 67   135
Audio track 68   136
Audio track 69   137
Audio track 70   137

Chapter 14: Three Into Two

Audio track 71   140
Audio track 72   141
Audio track 73   143

Chapter 15: Harmony

Audio track 74   145
Audio track 75   147
Audio track 76   150
Audio track 77   151
Audio track 78   153
Audio track 79   158

Introduction

Our aim in writing this book

This book is designed to be the first guide to reading (and writing) music notation that is written in plain English. We want to cut through the mystery and confusion surrounding music notation and make it as easy as possible for you to understand how it works. Yes, there's a bit of jargon along the way, but it will all be explained in simple, plain language.

Not only that, but for the first time we will use recordings to allow you to hear what individual bits of notation and music theory actually sound like. Every time you see an Audio Track icon in the sidebar, that means that there is an accompanying audio example that demonstrates something in the text. After all, how can you be expected to understand what music notation means if you can't hear the music that it represents?

All the audio examples can be found at this web address: **www.hybridpublications.com**. You'll also find all sorts of other supplementary material that will help you to get the most out of this book. For example, all the answers to the various exercises in the book are available there to download, along with lots of other extra material. Whenever extra material is available online you'll see this little "online material" logo in the sidebar.

Each chapter in the book ends with a worksheet which will test you on the various concepts and musical ideas introduced in that chapter. Worksheet answers can be found on pages 160–172. Again, extra reference material and worksheets can be found on the website.

Above all, we want to emphasise that learning to read music should be a practical activity and so we'll be encouraging you to play, sing and generally get involved in making music at every opportunity. It's only by putting the theory of music notation into practice that it will truly become second nature to you – and that's when you'll really start to get the most out of it. Good luck!

Hint and tips

Other interesting bits and pieces will be explained in tip boxes like this one. Look out for them throughout the book.

Audio track

Online material

Why learn to read music?

I'm assuming that if you've bought this book then you have some desire to learn to read music. But perhaps you're just browsing in a book shop or leafing though a copy at a friend's house – you may very well be wondering, "Why bother to learn to read music?".

There's no doubt that learning to read music is going to require real effort on your part. It's a logical and simple system, but it does require work and practice to master. And if you're going to put that work in, it's only reasonable to ask what the reward will be at the end of it.

Put simply, music notation is the common language of musicians all over the world. It's how we record, write down and communicate musical ideas. If you can read music, you can:

- write down your own musical ideas
- learn pieces or songs from sheet music
- play new music at sight
- communicate with other musicians around the world
- analyse and understand how music works

That's not to say that all musicians out there can read music. Particularly in the field of popular music, reading music notation is quite a rare skill. And depending on what you want to do, you might be able to get by without it. But if you want to make a living from music, improve your technique, write your own music or work with other musicians then there is no doubt that learning to read will make your musical life easier and more rewarding.

Think of a musician like a poet. A poet organises words and phrases into poems that can then be recited. In theory there is no need for a poet to be able to read – as long as he can recite his poems then he will be OK. But what does he do if he wants to record his poems, or to pass them on to other people to read and enjoy? At that point he (or she) needs to be able to write them down. Instead of words and phrases, the musician's tools are notes and rhythms, but he or she has the same need to record and communicate.

Bright idea

Why not talk to musicians you know and find out how they use music notation in their music-making activities? You might be surprised at the huge variety of musical styles and genres that it's used in.

What is music notation for?

In order to understand how music notation works, it's helpful to spend a couple of minutes thinking about what we, as musicians, need it to do. After all, it's a system that has been designed and developed by musicians over the years, so what is it designed to do?

In brief, music notation is designed to represent the key elements of music in as concise a way as possible. A musician playing a piece of music is involved in a complicated combination of tasks – we might be using both hands (and sometimes both feet) to work our instrument, playing hundreds of notes in precise rhythms often while trying to stay in time with other musicians. We need our system of notation to be as simple as possible – the last thing we need is anything too complicated.

So music notation has developed many forms of shorthand over the years to speed up the process of translating dots on the page into live music. It takes a while to get to grips with some of these conventions and shortcuts, but it's worth persevering because once you understand them they will actually make your life as a musician easier.

The type of notation that we're going to deal with in this book is (broadly speaking) based on Western classical music tradition. But that's not to say that this is the only type of notation that there is. For example, guitarists use a system of notation called tablature (developed from Renaissance lute notation) that specifies exactly where on the neck of the instrument each note is to be played.

Equally sol-fa notation was developed to help singers learn melodies without recourse to traditional music notation. Both these systems are perfectly valid and useful for their intended purposes. However, over the hundreds of years that Western music has been developing, the notation as described in this book has proved itself to be versatile and flexible enough to represent almost every type of music, from ballet music to heavy metal and from avante-garde classical music to pop songs. It's this flexibility that makes written music such a powerful tool.

Music history

Music notation, as we know it now, developed during the Middle Ages to help monks record religious music called *plainsong*. In its most basic form it was just a series of instructions specifying whether each note was higher or lower than the preceding one.

Music notation isn't perfect

There are hundreds (if not thousands) of variables that go into a musical performance – that's what makes live music so compelling, after all. It's important to realise that music notation isn't designed to record every single aspect of a performance, otherwise it would be so unwieldy and complicated as to be unusable.

Rather, music notation is designed to give us the basic musical facts; we, as musicians, are then expected to interpret these basic facts and turn them into real music. Music notation isn't music – it's just a set of instructions for how to create music, in the same way that a recipe isn't food.

If we wanted to create a complete description of music we might come up with something like the computer music language, MIDI. This is a standard way of describing music that computers and electronic musical instruments can understand. It catalogues and describes virtually every attribute of a piece of music in a ruthlessly scientific way, so that a computer can read back the instructions and recreate a piece of music.

Music notation's not like that – it's designed for humans to use and it only bothers to represent those elements of the music that are considered essential. The rest is up to you, and that's a big part of what makes being a musician so rewarding and satisfying.

So, as you work through this book always try to remember that written music is there to help you. At times it will seem like a ridiculously arcane system riddled with bizarre rules and traditions, and at times, it is. But those arcane rules and systems are all there for a reason and they've been refined and developed by generations of musicians.

So stick with it, and ultimately you'll be rewarded with access to an incredibly rich, flexible and concise system that will help you to achieve your musical goals, whatever they may be. Now, let's get started with the basics...

 Techno-tip

MIDI stands for **Musical Instrument Digital Interface** and was first developed in the 1980s. A "MIDI file" is a set of instructions that define note values, pitches, and many other parameters, which a computer can read and play back as music.

Chapter 1: The Basics

Before we start to worry about learning to read music notation, let's just take a couple of minutes to ask ourselves the question "What is music?". This may seem a simple question – after all we all recognise music when we hear it. But if we remember that the purpose of music notation is to provide instructions to musicians on how to recreate music, I think you'll agree that it's really important to understand what the end product is that we're trying to create. Think of music notation as a recipe, the musician as the chef and music itself as the finished dish – what we're really interested in is the taste of the end product!

At its most mechanical level music could be described as sound – waves of compression and rarefaction that are carried through the air to our ears, where they are converted into signals that our brains understand as music. But by this definition, the sound of a pneumatic drill or plane passing overhead would count as music, so there must be more to it than that.

OK, so maybe the question should be "What's the difference between sound and music?". Or to put it another way, what differentiates between Mozart and the sound of a drill or chainsaw? Well, Mozart spent a lot of time organising the various sounds at his disposal into a particular order – he arranged them to produce a certain effect that was pleasing to the ear.

Organised sound

Perhaps a good definition of music would be "organised sound"– this would cover everything from Bach to Drum'n'Bass, but would exclude noise and ambient sound. (Incidentally, this definition could also include speech, and there's a good deal of evidence to show that language and music are intimately connected.)

So, what are the basic elements of sound that we can manipulate, or organise, to create music? Well, let's think of the one musical instrument that we all possess – our voices. When we sing we can use our vocal cords to produce a number of different noises, and men

Is this music?

Check out some of these pieces of music to see just how wide the definition of music can be:

Edgar Varese: Ionisation
John Cage: 4'33"
Pierre Boulez: Le Marteau sans maître
My Bloody Valentine Glider
Anything by **Einstürzende Neubaten**

Online material

Visit **www.hybrid publications.com** for more listening ideas.

produce a different kind of noise to women. We tend to say that men's voices are *lower* than women's, and, conversely, that women's voices are *higher* than men's.

Pitch

When we use words like "higher" and "lower" to describe sounds what we are actually doing is describing the frequency of the sound wave (i.e. how many times per second it vibrates). A string vibrating very quickly produces a very high note, whereas one vibrating slowly produces a low note.

This is a fairly long-winded way of describing notes, so musicians use the word *pitch* to describe how high or low a note is. A women's voice is said to have a higher pitch than a man's voice. Alternatively, think of a piano keyboard; the notes on the left-hand side of the keyboard have a lower pitch than those on the right, and the pitch of the notes ascends gradually as we move from left to right.

Low pitch ⟶ High pitch

OK, so when we're singing we can vary the pitch of the notes to provide one element of organisation. What else do we have at our disposal? Well, when we speak or sing, we can choose how fast or slow we sing each note and for how long we hold it before we move onto the next one. We can also choose to leave gaps in a melody, for example to take a breath. When we make these decisions, what we are effectively doing is to organise sounds (notes) in time – we decide when each note should start and finish and how long it should be before the next one starts. Musicians call this element of organisation *rhythm*.

Techno tip

Pitch is equivalent to the scientific term *frequency*. The higher a note is, the higher its frequency. Frequency is measured in *hertz* (hz), and describes the number of oscillations of a sound wave per second.

Rhythm

Music is an artform that exists in time; musicians arrange sounds and pitches in time and that is what we call music. Rhythm is with us everywhere – in the patterns of speech, sounds of mechanical devices like trains or washing machines, patterns of human movements like running or walking and even in the sounds of the natural world like birdsong. So it should come as no surprise that rhythm is a vital part of music, and indeed, in some non-western musical cultures is far more important than pitch.

Pitch + Rhythm = Music

Well, not quite, as we'll see. But pitch and rhythm are the two key parts of music, and they are therefore the two key bits of information that music notation needs to communicate to the musician. The written music needs to tell us which notes to play, in which order, and when each one should start and stop. Let's start by looking at how music notation represents pitch.

Representing pitch

Let's go back to the piano keyboard on page 14. If you can, track down a piano and have a look inside. Whether it's an upright piano or a grand piano you'll see something similar – each key of the piano is connected via a complex mechanical system to a hammer. When you press down the key, this causes the hammer to strike a string (or group of strings) and this is what makes the sound. Here's a picture of the inside of a grand piano:

> **Musical quote**
>
> The UK comedian Eric Morecambe once famously answered criticism of his piano playing by quipping:
> "I *am* playing all the right notes, but not necessarily in the right order."

Imagine you're sitting at the piano keyboard looking at the strings – on the left-hand side they're very long and they get shorter as we move up. The longer, fatter strings correspond to the lowest notes on the keyboard while the shorter strings correspond to the higher notes. (This is because when the longer, fatter strings are struck by the hammer they vibrate more slowly than the higher, thinner strings, thus producing a lower note.)

If we were to represent the strings in a diagram, they might look a bit like this – a grid with lower notes on the left and higher notes on the right:

If you were looking at the strings from the side of the piano, the lower strings would be at the bottom of the grid and the higher, thinner strings would be at the top, like this

This seems like a pretty instinctive way of representing pitch: low notes are at the bottom and high notes are at the top. And in fact, music notation uses something very similar to this, called the *stave*.

Introducing the stave

The stave is a group of five horizontal lines that stretch from one side of the page to the other, like this:

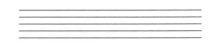

Just as with the "grid" diagram above, the lower the line the lower the pitch that it represents. By placing note symbols on this grid we can show exactly how high or low a note is.

Techno-tip

The speed at which a string vibrates is a function of its **length, tension** and **thickness**. For this reason, strings that produce low notes are long and thick, while those that create high notes are thin and short.

Let's start by putting some notes onto our grid:

Don't worry too much about the note symbols themselves for the time being, just look at how they are placed on the stave.

The first thing to notice is that we can place notes on any of the lines of the stave, as well as in the spaces between the lines. Notice too that the notes are arranged from left to right. We read music from left to right, just like text, so the music notation is telling us to play the notes in the order that we come across them. Or, to put it another way, the notes on the left are played before the notes on the right.

So, our system is coming together nicely. The only problem with this stave is that is only gives us relative information – it just tells us whether one note is higher or lower than another one. Ideally, we need to know *exactly* which note to play, so we need to identify one line on the stave and tell the musician which note it represents.

The clef

The *clef* is a symbol that will enable us to do exactly that. Have a look at the diagram below:

The clef is the little squiggly symbol that we've added at the start of the stave and it exists to identify one line of the stave as representing one unique note. In this case, notice how the squiggly shape centres around the second line up from the bottom.

This particular clef is sometime called the *G clef*, partly because it looks vaguely like a stylised capital G, but mostly because it tells us that this "encircled" line represents the note G (as we'll see shortly, notes are named after letters of the alphabet):

So, if we place a note on this line, we know that it represents the note G, which can be found on the piano keyboard here:

So what about the other notes on the keyboard, to the left and right of G? Well, all the white notes on the keyboard can be mapped onto the stave very simply; the notes to the right of G are placed in ascending order on the lines and spaces above G, and the notes to the left of G are placed in descending order on the lines and spaces below G, like this:

By placing these notes on the stave we can now locate all the following notes:

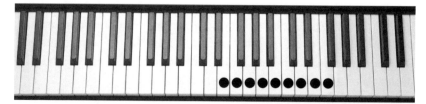

 Music fact

A more common name for the G clef is the *treble* clef. The range of notes that can be represented on this stave corresponds very closely to the range of notes that a boy can sing. In choral music, boys whose voices haven't broken are known as *trebles* – hence the name.

Naming the notes

Having identified the note G, we can now name the other notes on the stave. Just by taking a look at the piano keyboard you can see that there are a lot of notes to be named – it would be a big job to come up with unique names for every single note! So, musicians have come up with a simpler system, which just uses the first seven letters of the alphabet: A, B, C, D, E, F and G.

We already identified the letter G, so let's fill in some of the other names. To get the letter names of the notes below G, we just work backwards through the alphabet, like this:

Moving upwards from G is a little trickier. Because we've restricted ourselves to only using 7 letters we can't just call the next note H. In fact, we just start over again at A, like this:

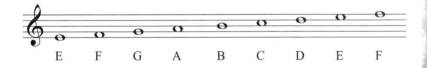

And here are these notes named on the keyboard:

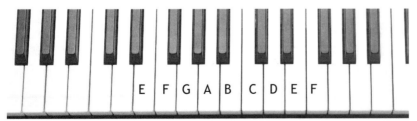

Eagle-eyed readers may have spotted that we now have two notes called E and two notes called F. Surely this is confusing? Actually, this is where the neatness of the 7-note naming system reveals itself...

Music fact

The note A, which is found in the second space of the treble stave, is the standard note that all orchestras tune to.
Before a concert, one of the players (usually the oboe player) plays an A, and all the other instruments tune to that note. The note A corresponds to a frequency of **440Hz.**

Introducing the octave

Count the number of notes on the stave between the two Es (including the Es themselves). You should find that there are eight notes. Notes that are eight notes apart have some very special properties in music and they have a lot in common, which is why we give them the same letter name. In fact, musicians give this eight-note spacing a special name – the *octave*.

Audio track 1

If you have access to a piano or keyboard try playing the two Es together, or listen to **Audio track 1**. They sound good together don't they?

Going even further...

Online material

Test your knowledge of note names with the musical Sudoku puzzles at **www.hybrid publications.com**

So we've now identified nine pitches on the stave and have given them each a letter-name. Let's look at the piano keyboard again and see where these notes are placed:

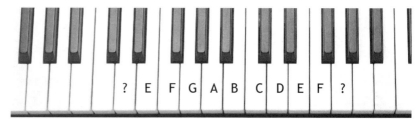

So what happens if we want to show a note that is above or below this group of notes on the keyboard? After all, there are plenty of other keys on the keyboard that don't seem to be included on the stave at the moment.

The science bit

The musical concept of the octave has a simple mathematical explanation. If we take a note and move it up an octave we **double** its frequency. Similarly if we move a note down an octave we **halve** its frequency.

Well, first of all, we can put notes above and below the top lines of the stave, so that one note is resting on the top line, and the other is hanging below the bottom line, like this:

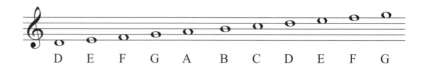

D E F G A B C D E F G

This has now extended the scope of the stave to 11 notes, but we can go even further. Think back to the inside of the piano, which had hundreds of strings, each one corresponding to one note. What we have constructed on our stave is basically a snap-shot of a section of these strings – 11 of them to be precise.

There's nothing to stop us extending the stave upwards and downwards almost indefinitely so that we can represent more and more notes above and below the set of 11 that we currently have. Musicians do this by adding small additional lines above or below the stave, called *ledger* lines.

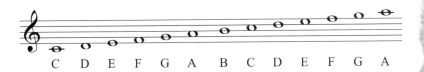

C   D   E   F   G   A   B   C   D   E   F   G   A

In the example above we've added a ledger line below and above the stave, which allows us to include the notes C and A (below and above the stave respectively). We can carry on adding more ledger lines to represent lower and higher notes.

The note C, which sits on the first ledger line below the stave, occupies a special place in most musician's minds as it is often the first note that pianists learn. This is for the simple reason that on most pianos it is found right in the middle of the keyboard, above the lock, and is therefore very easy to identify. It's known as middle C.

Moving on to rhythm

You've covered a huge amount of information on how we represent pitch in music notation, so now we're going to move on and look at some of the basics of rhythm.

Don't forget to try the worksheet at the end of this chapter to test yourself and check out **www.hybridpublications.com** for further downloadable resource sheets and test-yourself kits.

Readability

In practice, only a certain number of ledger lines are used, because they become quite difficult to read. Generally speaking you'll rarely see more than four ledger lines used above or below a stave. As we'll see later, we have other systems for representing notes beyond this range.

Online material

Visit **www.hybrid publications.com** for a full listing of notes on ledger lines.

Audio track 2

 Audio track 3

The basics of rhythm

We're going to look at rhythm in detail in the next chapter, but at this stage we'll introduce some of the basic concepts involved. Let's start with the most basic element of rhythm, the *pulse* or *beat*.

Feel the beat

The vast majority of music of all genres has at its heart a regular, repetitive pulse, which musicians call the *beat*. It's not a co-incidence that this resembles the name that we give our own inner pulse, the *heartbeat*. This is the most basic of all human rhythms, and when you consider that many types of music were written to accompany physical activities, be it dancing, walking, rowing or breaking rocks on a chain gang, the link between the regular beat of our hearts and the underlying pulse of music becomes very clear.

Listen to **Audio tracks 2** and **3**, both of which have strong, but contrasting pulses. Try tapping your foot, or clapping your hands in time. Try to notice how quickly you are tapping or clapping and whether or not some pulses are more important than others.

Groups of beats

As you tap along you will probably notice that the beats fall naturally into repetitive groups. In **Audio track 2**, the beats fall into groups of four, and in **Audio track 3**, they fall into groups of three.

Musicians call these groupings *bars*. A bar always contains the same number of beats, and the first beat of the bar is usually the most important. Try listening again to **Audio tracks 2** and **3** and this time count along like this:

Audio track 2: 1-2-3-4, **1**-2-3-4, **1**-2-3-4, etc.
Audio track 3: 1-2-3, **1**-2-3, **1**-2-3, **1**-2-3, etc.

Emphasise the "1" each time you come to it – this shows us where the bar starts and is vital for staying in time.

Bars and beats on the stave

Let's take a look at how these fundamental concepts are represented in music notation. Let's imagine that we are dealing with a piece that has four beats per bar. We'll indicate this by placing the number four at the beginning of the stave, just after the treble clef:

This number is known as a *time signature* – it tells us how many beats there are in a bar. Time signatures are actually a little more complicated than this, but this simpler version will be fine for us to use to start with. Now let's write in the 1-2-3-4 count to represent the four beats of each bar:

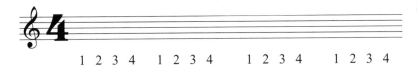

And finally, let's add some vertical lines to divide up each 1-2-3-4 count and show where each bar begins – these are called *bar lines*:

So our stave now contains the following information:

1. **Treble clef**   to tell us which note is which on the stave
2. **Time signature**   to tell us how many beats are in each bar
3. **Bar lines**   to show where each new bar begins

You're now ready to have a go at the worksheet overleaf, which will test you on all the ideas introduced in this chapter.

Worksheet 1 (answers on page 160)

1. Write these notes on the stave below (remember that some note names appear in two places on the stave):

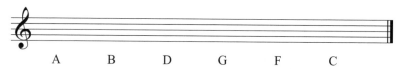

    A   B   D   G   F   C

2. Write the letter names of these notes under the stave:

3. Add notes on the stave to spell these three-letter words:

    E   G   G   A   D   D   B   A   G

4. Write down the letter names of these notes underneath the stave to form three more three-letter words:

5. Add a treble clef and time signature to this empty stave, and then add barlines to create two bars. Write a count of 1-2-3-4 under each bar:

6. What is the scientific term used to describe pitch?

Chapter 2: Rhythm

As we've seen, the two key elements of music that are communicated through music notation are pitch and rhythm. Many people find it relatively easy to understand the system of pitch notation – after all it's fairly instinctive; low notes are lower down and high notes are higher up.

However, rhythm notation is less intuitive and may take you a little longer to master; it has to do the tricky job of representing when events happen in time in a clear and concise way. Do persevere though because once you understand it, you'll find it invaluable in learning new music, communicating with other musicians and improving your own musicianship.

Listen and learn

Rhythms make most sense when we hear them; for example, most of us could clap back a drum pattern if it was played to us, even though we might have no idea about how to write it down. Once we've heard a rhythm demonstrated we find it easy to comprehend and repeat it.

In this book we'll use a "listen and learn" approach, using audio examples to demonstrate exactly how rhythms should sound. You'll be able to compare the sound of a rhythm with its equivalent notation, which will speed up the learning process.

As an example, listen to the rhythm that's demonstrated on **Audio track 4**. It's a two-bar rhythm played on the drums. After the rhythm is demonstrated there's a two-bar break for you to repeat it, then the rhythm will be repeated again. So, listen for two bars, then clap the rhythm back and finally listen again to the rhythm. After a few listens you'll probably find that you can clap the rhythm back accurately.

By the end of this chapter, you'll be able to write this rhythm down in music notation, and, perhaps more importantly, you'll be able to recognise it when written down, and repeat it.

Learning tip

Rhythmic patterns are incredibly important in all genres of music. Certain patterns crop up again and again and you'll soon start to recognise them. Once you do, you'll find it easier and easier to read rhythmic notation. Think of individual notes as being letters and rhythmic patterns as being words.

Audio track 4

Note values

As we saw back in Chapter 1, music is written down on a grid of five lines called a stave. On this stave we place symbols that represent musical notes. Most of you are probably familiar with some of the symbols that we use to represent notes. Each one represents a note of a different duration – some long and some short – and each has a different shape.

The semibreve

At the end of Chapter 1 we looked at an example with four beats in the bar, which we saw could be notated like this:

1 2 3 4   1 2 3 4   1 2 3 4   1 2 3 4

Now let's imagine that we want to write down a piece where one note is played in each bar, starting on the first beat and lasting for the whole bar. First of all we need a symbol that represents a note held for four beats; next, we place that symbol on the relevant stave line, at the beginning of the bar, like this:

Jargon buster

In the USA, the semibreve is called a *whole note*.

1 2 3 4   1 2 3 4   1 2 3 4   1 2 3 4

This note value is called a *semibreve* and it tells us that that note should be held for four beats, as shown by the 1-2-3-4 count.

This process can be repeated for the other three bars in the example, so that we have one semibreve in every bar, each one lasting for four beats.

And remember that we can place these semibreves anywhere we like on the stave, to represent different pitches:

This rhythm is demonstrated on **Audio track 5** – have a listen and try counting along. Listen to the rhythm of the piece and really try to feel the pulse and then count along evenly and steadily.

Audio track 5

Test yourself

Try adding semibreves to the following two examples. Make sure that you put the semibreve in the right place on the stave to create the note given below the stave.

Answers

Answers to all these exercises can be found at **www.hybrid publications.com**

Jargon buster

In the USA, the minim is known as the *half note*.

Up or down?

The stem of the minim can go either up or down. For notes above the middle line of the stave, the stem usually goes down. For notes below the middle line of the stave the stem goes up. Notes *on* the middle line can have stems that go up or down, depending on the other notes nearby.

Audio track 6

The minim

So, the semibreve note value allows us to write down notes that last for one complete bar of four beats. While this is certainly useful it doesn't make for particularly interesting rhythms, so we're going to need some more note values to liven things up a bit.

Let's start by chopping the semibreve in half. If a semibreve lasts for four beats and we divide it into two equal halves, then we should end up with two notes, each of which lasts for two beats.

1 semibreve =   2 minims

This new note is called a minim – it looks like a semibreve with a line sticking out of it, called a *stem*. It symbolises a note that lasts for two beats. In a bar of four beats, we will therefore need two minims to fill up the bar, like this:

1 2 3 4   1 2 3 4   1 2 3 4   1 2 3 4

Notice the positioning of each note in relation to the 1-2-3-4 count under the stave. The first minim starts on beat 1 and the second minim starts on beat 3, a pattern that is repeated in every bar.

As before, we can place these minims anywhere we like on the stave to introduce different pitches. The example below is demonstrated on **Audio track 6**. Have a listen and count along:

1 2 3 4   1 2 3 4   1 2 3 4   1 2 3 4

Test yourself

Here are some examples to get you using the semibreve and minim note values. Start by filling these bars with minims:

A   F   E   G   B   D   C   A

Now look at this example and see if you can fill in the missing notes:

A   C   B   G

Remembering note names

It's been a while since we introduced the names of the notes on the treble clef and you may be having trouble remembering them. Happily, over the years various tricks have been developed to help musicians remember which notes go where. Here are a couple that may help:

E   G   B   D   F   F   A   C   E

Notes on lines: **E G B D F**
Every **G**ood **B**oy **D**eserves **F**ootball

Notes on spaces: **F A C E** (spells FACE)

Add it up

Remember that each bar must contain a total of four beats. Semibreves are worth four beats and minims are worth two.

Answers

Answers to all these exercises can be found at **www.hybrid publications.com**

Jargon buster

A *mnemonic* is a phrase whose initial letters help you to remember something.

Jargon buster

In the USA, the crotchet is known as the *quarter note*. Getting the hang of the system yet?

The crotchet

If we can divide a semibreve in half to create a minim, what would happen if we divided a minim in half? Remember, we divided the 4-beat semibreve in half to create the 2-beat minim; if we divide that note in half again we'll create a note that is worth 1 beat, which we call a *crotchet*.

1 semibreve =   2 minims =   4 crotchets

A crotchet lasts for one beat, and looks similar to a minim, except that the notehead is filled in. In a four-beat bar, we'll need four crotchets to fill it up, like this:

Of course we can place crotchets anywhere on the stave to represent different pitches, and, just like the minim, the crotchet's stem can flip up or down depending on where on the stave it occurs. For notes above the middle line the stem goes down; for notes below the middle line the stem goes up. For notes on the middle line, the stem can go either up or down, depending on the other notes around it.

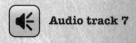**Audio track 7**

The example above is demonstrated on **Audio track 7**. Have a listen and count along – remember that each crotchet lasts for one beat only. If you have access to a piano, keyboard or other instrument, trying playing along with the notes.

Test yourself

We've now got three different note values that we can mix up to produce different rhythms. This is already enough to produce a bewildering variety of different rhythmic patterns. Try the following exercises, which use semibreves, minims and crotchets and remember that each bar must contain four beats.

In this exercise fill in each gap with one note to make the bar add up to four beats:

Here, add crotchets at the correct pitch to spell out these four letter words – make sure that all your crotchet note-heads are filled in and that all your stems are going in the right direction!

B E A D   F A C E   D E A D   F A D E

In this exercise, try to come up with three possible ways of arranging a minim and two crotchets in a bar.

Then try clapping all three rhythms while counting out loud. Keep the counting steady and regular and don't be put off by the different rhythms. Try getting gradually speeding up to see how fast you can do it!

Answers

Answers to all these exercises can be found at **www.hybrid publications.com**

Beat values

Semibreve	**4**
Minim	**2**
Crotchet	**1**

Stem directions

Below middle line
Up
Above middle line
Down
On middle line
Up or down

Audio track 8

The quaver

With the crotchet we have a note value that is equal to one beat. Let's divide that in half again to create a new note value that is worth half a beat, the quaver:

1 semibreve =   2 minims =   4 crotchets =   8 quavers

The quaver looks a bit like the crotchet in that it has a filled-in notehead and a stem; however, it also has a squiggly shape on the end of the stem that we call the *tail*.

All the note values that we've come across so far have been expressed in numbers of beats; but the quaver is shorter than one beat so how do we count it? Very simply – we just put the word "and" in between each beat, like this (listen to **Audio track 8** to hear it demonstrated):

1   &   2   &   3   &   4   &

Sometimes, when a bunch of quavers occur together they can be difficult to read. So, if we need to, we can join up the tails of the quavers to group them together, making them easier to understand:

The tails are joined together into a thicker line called a *beam*. Quavers are usually beamed in groups of two or four – it doesn't make any difference at all to how they are played, it's just for neatness.

Test yourself

We've now got four different note values that we can mix up to produce different rhythms. I hope that you can already see the huge variety of rhythms that could be created using just these four. Try the following exercises, which use semibreves, minims, crotchets and quavers – as before, remember that each bar must add up to four beats.

In this exercise fill in each gap with one note to make the bar add up to four beats:

Here, add groups of crotchets and two quavers at the correct pitch to spell out these three letter words – beam each group of two quavers together and try to get the stems in the right direction. (Where notes appear in two places on the stave , use the higher option in each case.)

D A D, B E D, A G E, B E E, C A B, F E D

In this exercise, try to come up with three possible ways of arranging two crotchets and four quavers in a bar.

Write the counts out under the stave, making sure that you use an "&" for the quavers. Then try clapping all three rhythms while counting out loud. Keep the counting steady and regular and don't be put off by the different rhythms. Try gradually speeding up to see how fast you can do it!

The semiquaver

For the last time we're going to divide by two to create a new note value – this time we're chopping the quaver in half to create the *semiquaver*:

4 crotchets = 8 quavers =   16 semiquavers

Just as a crotchet contains two quavers, so a quaver contains two semiquavers. Or to put it another way, a crotchet is the equivalent of four semiquavers.

The semiquaver looks very similar to the quaver, the only difference being an extra tail. Just like the quaver, the semiquaver can be beamed together in groups of two or four.

Counting the semiquaver

The semiquaver can be tricky to count as it is the shortest note that you are likely to come across, and four of them fit into one beat. The best way to count semiquavers is:

1-a-&-a, **2**-a-&-a, **3**-a-&-a, **4**-a-&-a,

Try counting along with this example, which can be heard on **Audio track 9**. The piece is quite slow, so the notes won't go by as quickly as you might think. Count steadily and evenly throughout;

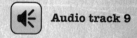

Audio track 9

Don't panic if you can't get this straight away – try counting the rhythm out yourself slowly and then gradually speed up.

Test yourself

In this exercise fill in each gap with one note to make the bar add up to four beats:

Beat values

Semibreve	**4**
Minim	**2**
Crotchet	**1**
Quaver	**1/2**
Semiquaver	**1/4**

Complete the missing spaces in this example with groups of semiquavers, according to the letter names below the stave:

Answers

Answers to all these exercises can be found at **www.hybrid publications.com**

D E F G   D C B A   E F G A

Summary of note values

Congratulations! You've now learned all five note values that you will need to complete this book. Other note values do exist, but it's unlikely that you will come across them in the early stages of reading music notation. Here's a quick summary of the note values you've learned, their symbols and how to count them:

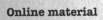

Online material

Visit **www.hybrid publications.com** for a complete reference guide to note values.

Worksheet 2 (answers on page 161)

1. Add one note to each bar to make the total number of beats add up to four:

2. Add note values to the stave according to the number of beats written below. We've done the first one for you:

3. This example contains one bar of unbeamed quavers and semiquavers. Copy the same rhythm into the second bar, adding beams as necessary:

4. Use crotchets to spell out these three-letter words, making sure that the stems point in the correct direction. Where you have a choice of position for a note on the stave, always choose the higher of the two:

5. What are the US terms for the following note values?
a. Quaver
b. Semibreve
c. Crotchet
d. Semiquaver

Answers

Answers to this worksheet can be found on page 161.

Online material

Additional worksheets are available at **www.hybrid publications.com**.

Online material

Visit **www.hybrid publications.com** for an interactive rhythm test.

Chapter 3: Sound & Silence

You've now got a lot of the tools that you need to understand music notation. You know how to represent pitch, and you've got five note values that you can use to construct different rhythmic patterns. There's just one vital piece of the jigsaw missing...

In music, as we've already discovered, you are told which notes to play, and in what rhythm to play them. But you also need to be told when *not* to play, because all music has periods of rest, or silence.

In fact, when it comes to playing music, what you don't play is just as important as what you do play. Imagine a melody with no breaks or pauses in it – it would be inexorable, unmusical and unpleasant. As we've said before, music and language are very closely linked and we use breaks and periods of silence in our speech to (literally) punctuate what we are saying. It's exactly the same in music – apart from anything else, singers and woodwind and brass players need spaces in the music during which they can breathe.

Rests

The way silence is treated in music is very similar to the way that sound is treated – we need to know when to be silent and for how long. On one level at least it is simpler, because we don't need to worry about pitch!

In fact, music notation contains special symbols called *rests*, which behave in exactly the same way to note values. For each of the five note values that you've learned in Chapter 2, there is an equivalent rest. Just as a minim note tells you to play for two beats, a minim rest tells you to be silent for two beats. By combining note values and rests together we will finally create the essential elements that you need to understand rhythm in music.

In this chapter we will introduce each of the five rests and show how they can be combined with the note values that you already know to create some interesting rhythmic patterns.

Online material

Visit **www.hybrid publications.com** for more listening ideas.

Don't relax!

The word "rest" implies an element of relaxation or lessening of concentration. In fact, nothing could be further from the truth: rests need to be counted and observed just as carefully as notes.

The semibreve rest

As you'll recall from Chapter 2, the semibreve note lasts for four beats. It will come as no surprise to discover, therefore, that the semibreve rest also lasts for four beats. Here's an example showing both notes and rests:

Semibreve   Semibreve rest

The first thing to note (if you'll forgive the pun) is that the semibreve rest looks nothing like the semibreve note (this is true for all the notes and their equivalent rests). The semibreve rest is a small, filled-in rectangle that hangs from the fourth line of the stave.

It's important to remember that rests should be counted just as carefully as notes. Many beginners make the mistake of "switching off" when they come across a rest, only to discover that they're not then prepared for their next note.

Semibreve rests should therefore be counted in exactly the same way as semibreve notes, as the counts under this next example show:

1 2 3 4   1 2 3 4   1 2 3 4   1 2 3 4

This example is demonstrated on **Audio track 10**. Have a listen and then count along, paying special attention to counting the rests.

Note that when counting the four beat notes, the note starts on beat 1 and is then held all the way through beats 2, 3 and 4 stopping at exactly the point that you count beat 1 again. A common mistake is to come off on beat 4, which would make the note only 3 beats long.

The minim rest

Here's the rest that is equivalent to the minim, lasting for two beats:.

Minim   Minim rest

Once again the rest looks nothing like its equivalent note. This time the minim rest looks like a small filled-in rectangle placed on top of the third line of the stave.

It can be difficult to remember which rest is the minim rest and which is the semibreve. Here's a little trick to help it stick in your memory: it's harder for a rest to hang from a line (as the semibreve rest does) than it is for a rest to sit on the line (as the minim rest does). Similarly, it's harder to hold a note for four beats than it is to hold one for two beats. Therefore the rest hanging from the lines represents four beats and the rest sitting on the line represents two beats. Easy!

As before, remember that it's just as important to count rests as it is to count notes. This example uses both semibreve and minim rests:

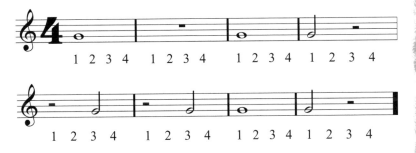

This example is demonstrated on **Audio track 11**. Listen carefully and then have a go at counting along with it. Note that semibreve and minim rests are placed slightly differently in the bar. Because the semibreve rest is frequently used to denote a whole bar's rest it is usually placed in the centre of the bar. The minim rest, however, usually appears above the 1st or 3rd beat, as above.

Two staves

This is the first example we've seen that goes over from one stave to two. Read the first stave from left to right as usual; once you get to the right-hand end, just move onto the stave below, starting again on the left-hand side. It's just like reading text.

Audio track 11

The crotchet rest

The crotchet, or one-beat rest, not only looks nothing like its note counterpart but also nothing like the other two rests we've encountered so far. Here's an example showing both crotchet notes and rests:

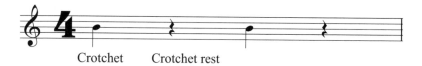

Crotchet   Crotchet rest

Resembling a calligraphic squiggle, the crotchet rest sits in a central position on the stave, although it can move higher or lower than this if necessary (due to the position of other notes or rests).

The crotchet rest is probably the easier of all the rests to count. Here are a couple of examples to get you started:

1   2   3   4   1   2   3   4   1   2   3   4   1   2   3   4

1   2   3   4   1   2   3   4   1   2   3   4   1   2   3   4

Rest shape

It can take a while to get to grips with drawing the crotchet rest. Start at the top of the rest and draw a zig-zag line of three segments and then finish off with a "C" shape.

Audio track 12

This second exercise is demonstrated on **Audio track 12**. You should find counting along with this relatively straightforward, so once you feel secure, try singing the melody or playing it on your instrument of choice. Take special care over the endings of notes before rests – the note should be held right up to the moment you count the beat that the rest appears on. For example, if you were playing a minim you can try counting 1-2-OFF to ensure that you come off the note at the correct time.

The quaver rest

The quaver rest is particularly versatile and can be used to create some intriguing rhythmic patterns, throwing the rhythmic emphasis away from the main beats of the bar.

Quaver Quaver rest

The quaver rest looks a little like an elaborate number seven and sits in the centre of the stave. Unlike its note counterpart it has no stem or tail and there is no need to beam quaver rests together. If two quaver rests appear together they can simply be replaced by a crotchet rest; four quavers together can be replaced by a minim rest.

Counting quaver rests can be tricky. One good trick is to count quavers as before, but when you get to a rest replace the number you are counting (or the "&" you are counting) with the word OFF. For example the opening bar of the following exercise would be counted:

1-&-2-OFF-3&4-OFF

1 & 2 off 3 & 4 off   1 & 2 off 3 & 4 off

1 & 2 off 3 & 4 off   1 & 2 & 3 4

This example is demonstrated on **Audio track 13**, complete with suggested counting. Try counting along yourself and then try singing or playing the melody. If you have trouble getting the rests in the right places then slow the speed right down and practice it really slowly until you are secure; only then should you try to speed it up.

Audio track 13

The semiquaver rest

For the sake of completeness we will show you the semiquaver rest here, although we won't be using it in any of the exercises at this stage. Lasting a quarter of a beat, it is often used in more complex rhythmic patterns, usually in conjunction with its equivalent note:

Similar to the quaver rest, but with an additional bar, the semiquaver rest sits in the centre of the stave.

Summary of rest and note values

This table summarises all the rest and note values that you've learned so far. These are the only rest and note values that will be used in this book so make sure that you know each symbol and how they are counted.

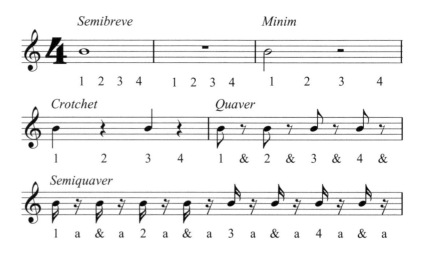

Rest values

As a general rule, the more squiggly a rest the shorter its value. Semibreve and minim rests are very plain, while the semiquaver rest is quite intricate.

Online material

Download a complete reference guide to note and rest values at **www.hybrid publications.com**

42

Test yourself

Here are three examples using a variety of the rest and note values that you've learned so far. In each case the rhythmic pattern is demonstrated on the **Audio track** associated with each example.

Listen to the **Audio track** and follow the notation, counting along with the track. Then try to clap the rhythm back, counting out loud. Finally, then try to sing or play the example back again without listening to the audio.

Audio track 14

Audio track 15

Audio track 16

In the next chapter we're going to return to the world of pitch, so make sure that you have understood everything in this chapter and the previous chapter before you move on. As we move through the book, future chapters will build on the information in these earlier chapters so it is really worth spending as much time as it takes to understand these basic principles properly.

The worksheet overleaf will help you to test your knowledge. Remember that extra worksheets and test-yourself materials are available online at **www.hybridpublications.com**.

Worksheet 3 (answers on page 162)

1. Add one rest to each bar to make the total number of beats add up to four:

2. Add rests in the gaps to make the total number of beats in each bar add up to four:

Answers

Answers to this worksheet can be found on page 162.

3. Join up the rest values with their equivalent note values:

♪	▬
♬	▬
𝅗𝅥	𝄾
𝅝	𝄿
𝅘𝅥	𝄽

Online material

Additional worksheets are available at **www.hybrid publications.com**.

4. Add quaver rests to make up the correct number of beats in each bar:

Online material

Visit **www.hybrid publications.com** for an interactive rhythm test.

5. How many semiquaver rests could be fitted into one bar of four beats?

Chapter 4: Accidentals

Let's leave rhythm for a while and return to the world of pitch, where there is much more to learn. At the end of Chapter 1, we had introduced the concept of the stave, with notes placed on or between lines, or on ledger lines.

To refresh your memory here is a staff complete with all the pitches that we have encountered so far:

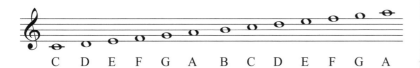

C D E F G A B C D E F G A

And here is where they can be found on the piano keyboard:

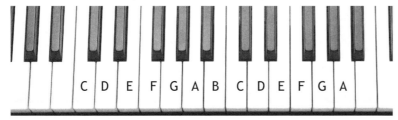

Notice anything strange?

We know that there are lots of notes above and below our collection of pitches, and we've shown how ledger lines can be used to notate some of these. In fact, there are other, more convenient ways of writing these pitches, which we'll introduce later in this book.

But before we get onto that, there are some other notes on the piano keyboard that we haven't represented on our stave – the black notes. Inbetween the 11 white notes that are already sitting on our stave are five black notes. But we don't have any room on our stave for these new notes – all the lines and spaces are filled up.

In this chapter we'll show you how to represent these notes on the stave with an ingenious system of symbols called *accidentals*.

Online material

Historical fact

On early keyboard instruments the white and black keys were the other way round. The main keys of the instrument were black, and the intervening keys were white.

Let's start by looking at the pattern of white and black notes on the keyboard. It's slightly odd, because the black notes don't occur between every white note – only some of them:

 Hint

The irregular pattern of black keys on the keyboard is actually quite useful when it comes to finding notes on the keyboard. For example, the white note immediately to the left of the group of two black keys is always C, while the white note immediately to the left of the group of three black keys is always F.

Looking at the keyboard diagram above, you'll see that we have black notes just to the right of the notes C, D, F, G and A, forming a pattern of three black notes, then two. This pattern is repeated across the whole length of the keyboard. Let's suppose that we wanted to locate the note indicated below:

One possible way of doing this would be to say: "Find the note C, then move upwards to the black note immediately to the right of it". This is the basis of the system called accidentals.

In fact, we use a symbol that looks like this: # as a shortcut for "move upwards to the black note to the right of it". You may recognise this symbol from your telephone keypad, where it's called a hash sign; however, musicians call it a *sharp* symbol. So the note indicated on the keyboard diagram above would be called C#, or C sharp.

Using the same system, we can now name all five black notes:

C# (C sharp):   black note immediately above C
D# (D sharp):   black note immediately above D
F# (F sharp):   black note immediately above F
G# (C sharp):   black note immediately above G
A# (C sharp):   black note immediately above A

When it comes to writing sharps on the stave, we use exactly the same symbol, but place it before the note that we want to affect. So the stave below shows how to turn C into C sharp – or to put it another way, the C has been *sharpened*:

So you can see how the sharp symbol allows us to use one space on the stave to represent more than one note. When the sharp symbol is written on the stave, the central "square" of the symbol should sit centrally between the two lines. When a sharp is written on a line, the "square" should be centred on the line. Here's what the other black notes look like when written on the stave:

And finally, here's the complete collection of notes, and the piano keyboard – you should now be able to see that we can relate every note on the keyboard to a symbol on the stave:

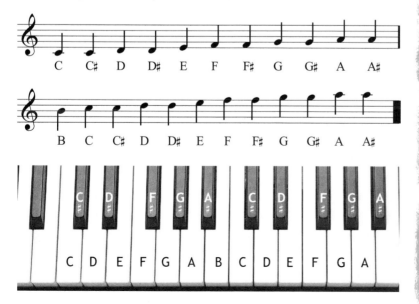

Pause for thought

Let's just stop for a second to gather our breath and consider what we've now achieved. We now know how to represent every single note on the piano keyboard: on the stave, we can write the notes D to E (including the black notes), and then by using ledger lines we can extend this system above and below as necessary. So, in theory, you can now represent any note in music notation – that's pretty cool!

Audio track 17

Let's take a look at all the notes between middle C, which you'll remember sits on the first ledger line below the stave and the C one octave above it. Listen to **Audio track 17** to hear what it sounds like:

Music fact

These 12 notes are known as the *chromatic scale*. The root of this word, *chroma*, means colour, and we can use some of these notes to add *harmonic colour* to melodies and chord progressions.

Notice that there are 12 notes from middle C before we reach the C one octave above. These 12 notes form the basis of all Western music – that's everything from Bach to the Beatles, from Classical to Punk and from a sweeping orchestral theme to a four-to-the-floor techno track.

But hang on a minute – how can only 12 notes create the huge variety of styles of music that we hear every day? Surely there are only a limited number of possible melodies? Eventually, all possible combinations of these notes must be used up, right?

Well, there *are* a limited number, but that number is incredibly vast. Just think about the number of possible variations: firstly, our 12 notes can be played in any octave – the average piano keyboard contains eight octaves, so we've immediately increased our pool of available notes to 96. Then they can be played in any order, and in any rhythmic pattern and at any speed. Let's assume that one musical phrase contains only four notes – this still means that there are nearly 85 million possible combinations of these 96 notes. Even allowing for the fact that some of these combinations won't sound very good that's plenty to be going on with.

Then of course these notes can be played on any instrument at any volume and in any style. And that's before we've even started to think about adding an accompaniment or words to our melody, which could distinguish it further. It turns out that there are literally billions and billions of possible combinations of notes, and that's why composers and writers can keep coming up with new melodies.

Tones and semitones

The pattern of 12 white and black notes on the piano keyboard and stave looks a little random, with its uneven spacing and clumps of black notes. However, this isn't really the case. Musicians actually think of each note as being the same distance away from its nearest neighbour. So C is the same distance from C# as F is from F# and B is from C:

In fact, you can think of our group of 12 notes as a regularly spaced grid, like this:

C	C#	D	D#	E	F	F#	G	G#	A	A#	B	C

The musical "distance" between each note is called a *semitone*. So, C is a semitone away from C# (and vice versa) and F is a semitone away from F#. In fact, another way of describing the sharp sign would be as an instruction that says "Raise this note by one semitone".

If we were to move from C to D, or from F# to G#, we would describe that as a distance of two semitones, or one *tone*.

Jargon buster

In the USA, tones and semitones are sometimes referred to as *steps* and *half-steps*.

Keeping sharp

Here are a few examples to make sure that you've really understood the concept of sharps and semitones. Start with this one; look at the notes indicated on the piano keyboard and then write them on the stave.

Now raise each of the notes shown on the stave below by one semitone and write them on the stave:

Finally, look at the groups of two notes on the stave below and write underneath them the distance between them in semitones. We've done the first one for you:

1 semitone

Refer back to the diagram of semitones on page 49 if you need help.

Looking at things the other way round

Some of you may have spotted that there is another way of looking at the system of accidentals that we've outlined on the preceding pages. Surely, if we can use the sharp sign to indicate notes that are a semitone higher, there should be another sign that indicates notes that are a semitone *lower*? After all, the black note a semitone higher than G could also be described as the black note that is a semitone lower than A.

As it happens, there *is* another musical sign, which is effectively the opposite of the sharp sign. In the real world, the opposite of "sharp" would be "blunt"; however, here (as in many other areas) musicians like to be different and the musical symbol that is opposite to the sharp is called a *flat*. The flat symbol looks like a slightly squashed "b", and just like the sharp sign, it is placed before the note that it refers to:

B   B♭

The flat symbol is an instruction that tells us to *lower* a note by a semitone. Looking at the piano keyboard, we can see that the black note indicated is a semitone below B, and therefore we can describe it as B flat:

Alternatively, we could describe it as A sharp. The decision on whether to call it B flat or A sharp depends on the musical context at the time. Sometimes it's more helpful to think of it as a flat and other times it's more helpful to think of it as a sharp.

Errr?

What happens if we put a sharp sign in front of a note that doesn't have a black note immediately above it, like E, for example? Well, we still follow the same rule and move up one semitone, which takes us from E to F. So, E sharp is another way of writing the note F. They amount to the same thing.

Here's how we would write the five black notes as flats:

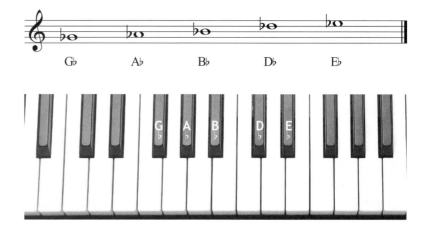

And finally, here's the complete set of 12 notes, written out using flats instead of sharps;

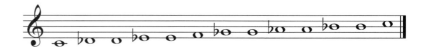

Intonation

If you spend much time hanging around with musicians (which many people advise against) you'll probably hear them say to one another "That note was a bit flat" or "You're going sharp towards the end". Here they're using the words flat and sharp to refer to small increments in pitch, downwards and upwards respectively.

Remember that pitch is a continuous curve – there are an infinite number of pitches, but we as musicians have developed a system that divides this continuous spectrum into octaves and semitones. If a singer sings a note that is slightly below one of these defined semitones we say that he or she is singing "flat"; likewise, if the note is pitched slightly too high, we describe it as sharp. The art of hitting notes accurately is called *intonation* and is a particular problem for singers.

💡 **Errr, again**

And the same thing applies to flats – F flat is the same note as E, and C flat is the same note as B. This fact does come in useful (honestly) but it's beyond the scope of this book...

Flats in practice

Let's take a look at how the flat sign is used in practice. Here's an example using note values that you learned in Chapters 2 and 3:

Audio track 18

You can hear what this sounds like on **Audio track 18**. Notice how the flat sign sits just before the note that it refers to, centred on the same line or space.

Here are a couple of examples for you to try. To start with, write these notes on the keyboard as flats on the stave:

Keep it tidy

Remember to place the flat or sharp sign on the same line or space as the note that it affects. The flat or sharp signs should sit neatly just before the note – not too close, but near enough that there is no ambiguity about which note the accidental refers to.

Write the note names under each note.

In this example, write flat signs in front of all the Bs and Es to turn them into B flats and E flats:

Answers

Answers to all these exercises can be found at **www.hybrid publications.com**

Keeping it tidy

Take a look at the example below. Here we've used flat signs in every bar to show that all the As, Bs and Es should be played as A flats, B flats and E flats. This means that there are an awful lot of flat signs flying around, which makes the music notation look complicated.

Music notation is all about giving instructions to musicians in the simplest possible way, and so we often find ways to simplify these instructions, to make life as easy as possible for the musician who is reading the notes.

In this case, we'd like to reduce the number of flat signs on the page, because they're cluttering up the music and making it difficult to read. So, we introduce a little rule, which says:

"In any given bar, if a note has an accidental in front of it, then that accidental applies to all notes of that pitch in that bar"

So, if we apply this rule to the example above, the music notation would look like this:

Much clearer, I think you'll agree. In the first bar, the first E flat is marked as normal, but the second E flat, on beat two, doesn't need a flat sign, because the flat at the beginning of the bar still applies. Similarly, in the second half of the same bar, the flat sign before the B on beat three also affects the B on beat four.

Have a go yourself. Here's an example that includes lots of flats. Try writing it out again, but only add a flat to a note the first time it occurs in a bar:

This rule can also be applied to sharps. Here's a similar exercise – this time simplify the example below by removing any unnecessary sharp signs:

Remember that at the end of each bar, all the accidentals in that bar "expire" and no longer apply to notes in the following bar. We start each bar with a "clean slate" and any notes that were sharpened or flattened in the previous bar that we want to continue to be sharp or flat, need to have their respective accidental signs restated. This sounds complicated, but don't worry – it will soon become second nature!

The clean slate

At the end of each bar, the "slate" is wiped clean and all the accidentals in that bar are forgotten. We start the next bar with a clean "slate".

Answers

Answers to all these exercises can be found at **www.hybrid publications.com**

Sharps, flats – and naturals

The "one bar" rule for accidentals saves us a lot of time and effort when reading or writing music notation. However, it does create one problem; supposing we have a melody which, within the space of one bar, requires a pitch with an accidental, followed by the same pitch without one.

In the example below, the B on the first beat of the second bar is flattened. As it currently stands the'"one bar" rule tells us that the B on the fourth beat of the bar should therefore also be flattened:

But what do we do if we don't want the second B to be flattened? Well, we introduce our third accidental symbol, the *natural* sign. We can place this sign, (which looks like this: ♮) in front of the second B to cancel the B flat from earlier in the bar:

The natural sign tells us; "I know this note should be flattened/sharpened because of an accidental earlier in the bar, but I want you to ignore that and play the note in its unflattened / unsharpened form". And I think you'll agree that using the natural sign is a lot neater than writing that out every time.

With these three signs, collectively known as *accidentals*, we can represent every possible pitch on the stave in a clear and easily readable way. As we'll see in Chapter 7, we can go even further in simplifying the use of accidentals on the stave, but for the time being this is as much as you need to know.

The natural

Just like the flat and sharp signs, the natural sign is centred on the line or space of the note to which it refers.

So far, all the examples we've looked at have used flats and naturals, or sharps and naturals. But there's no reason why sharps, flats and naturals cannot be used within the same piece, or even within the same bar, as this example shows:

Listen to **Audio track 19** to hear what this sounds like – notice how the feel of the music is affected by the accidentals. They add a new palette of musical colour and allow composers and songwriters to take melodies in new and exciting directions.

There's a lot to keep track of here, but the basic rules governing accidentals are very simple, and can be summarised like this:

- Sharps raise a note by a semitone
- Flats lower a note by a semitone
- Accidentals last for a bar
- Naturals cancel out preceding accidentals in that bar

Further exploration

That's as far as we're going with our exploration of pitch, for the time being. But if you'd like to find out more, why not try some of these suggestions and explore further.

- Try writing your own melodies. Perfect them on a keyboard, sing them, or play them on your own instrument and then try writing them down.

- Check out the further examples and exercises available online at **www.hybridpublications.com**

- Look at sheet music to see how accidentals are used. If you can, find a recording and try to follow the melody as you listen.

Audio track 19

Why not?

Test your understanding of flats by writing out the chromatic scale on page 47 using flats instead of sharps.
Hint: you'll need to use five flat signs.

Online material

Visit **www.hybrid publications.com** for a complete reference guide to accidentals.

Worksheet 4 (answers on page 163)

1. Write these notes on the stave below:

C♯   A♭   E♭   F♯   B♭   G♯

2. Next to each note given below write another note that is a semitone higher:

3. Next to each note given below write another note that is a tone higher. Use sharp symbols where necessary:

4. Simplify this example, removing any unnecessary sharps and flats:

5. How would you express these notes using flat signs?

a. C♯

b. F♯

c. A♯

d. G♯

e. D♯

Answers

Answers to this worksheet can be found on page 163.

Online material

Additional worksheets are available at **www.hybrid publications.com**.

Online material

Visit **www.hybrid publications.com** for an interactive pitch test.

Chapter 5:
Put It Together

We've covered a huge amount of material in the first four chapters of this book and you've now learned all the basics of pitch and rhythm. The new information has been coming thick and fast, so in this chapter we're going to take a breather, review all of the material that we've covered so far, and show you how it can be used in real musical situations.

Remember that music notation is primarily a tool to enable musicians to communicate with each other. It's not an end in itself – it's there to improve your music making and it should always be related back to practical musical activities.

Don't panic!

Over the last 58 pages, we've introduced loads of different symbols, musical terms and other bits of jargon. It's entirely understandable if you're having trouble remembering which notes go where on the stave, or what a particular note value or rest looks like.

If you go to **www.hybridpublications.com** you'll find quick reference guides to musical terms, pitch and rhythm, so if you're stuck you can always refer back to them – you'll also find loads of other downloadable resources that will help you.

Or why not try something more creative – for example, why not make flash cards with note and rest values on them and play a game of musical snap? Get friends and family to test you, and make sure you're rewarded when you get everything right! Above all, listen to as much music as you can and try to relate what you've learned back to pieces that you know, and songs and tunes that you love.

I can't emphasise enough how important it is that you understand the basic concepts of music notation before you go any further. All of the material that appears later in this book builds on the concepts introduced in Chapters 1–4. If you're unsure about anything, find a friendly local musician and ask them to explain it to you again.

Write it out

If you're having trouble remembering note values or pitches on the stave then try writing them out over and over again. Just the act of writing them out will make them easier to remember.

Online material

Why not visit **www.hybrid publications.com** and download our flashcard templates? All the note values and rests that we've covered so far are included, plus other key musical symbols. There's even space for you to add your own!

Rhythm workout

Let's start by reviewing some of the rhythmic notation that we covered back in Chapters 2 and 3. Here are some basic note values – in each case work out how many of the notes in the second column it would take to make the note in the first column. We've done the first one for you.

1x	𝅝	=	8x	♪
4x	♩	=		♪
8x	♪	=		𝅗𝅥
4x	𝅗𝅥	=		𝅝
6x	♪	=		♩

Now try filling in the gaps in this rhythmic pattern; in each case there is one note missing:

And now try writing out this rhythmic pattern according to the numbers below the stave; each number tells you how many beats should be allocated to that note.

Remember that quavers and semiquavers in groups should be beamed together! Refer back to pages 47–57 if necessary..

 Add it up

Remember that the number of beats in a bar must always add up to the number given by the time signature.

 Answers

Answers to these exercises can be found at **www.hybrid publications.com**

Now let's move on to some exercises featuring rests. As on the previous page, fill in this table to show how many rests you would need in the second column to make the rest value in the first column:

Beat values

Semibreve	4
Minim	2
Crotchet	1
Quaver	1/2
Semiquaver	1/4

2X	𝄿	=		𝄾
4X	𝄽	=		𝄻
1X	𝄻	=		𝄿
2X	𝄻	=		𝄽
8x	𝄾	=		𝄻

Now join up each note value with its equivalent rest value. Refer back to pages 47–57 if necessary.

Answers

Answers to all these exercises can be found at **www.hybrid publications.com**

♪	𝄿
𝅘𝅥𝅯	𝄽
𝅗𝅥	𝄻
𝅝	𝄻
♩	𝄾

Next, fill in the gaps in this rhythmic pattern with rests:

And finally, clap back this rhythm. Sound familiar? Check against **Audio track 20** to see if you got it right.

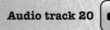

Audio track 20

Pitch workout

Now let's review all the information you've learned on pitch. Let's start with some simple note-naming exercises. Firstly, write these notes on the stave. (Remember that some of these notes can be found in more than one place on the stave!)

Next up, write the letter names of these notes under the stave to spell out two four-letter words:

Here are four notes written on the stave. In each case follow these notes with another note a semitone above.

Hint: some of these will require the use of the sharp symbol, but others won't!

Finally, using flat signs fill in the gaps in this exercise so that there is a semitone between every pair of notes:

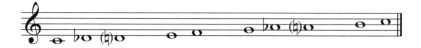

Now let's combine pitch and rhythm and see how you get on.

In this example, there are gaps left in the melody. The letter names below the stave tell you which note needs to be added, but you will have to work out what note value fits. If there is a * below the stave then add a rest of the appropriate length:

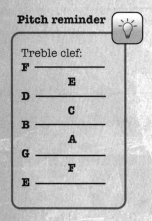

Pitch reminder

Treble clef:

F ——————
E
D ——————
C
B ——————
A
G ——————
F
E ——————

E   *   A   G E

Here's another similar exercise:

C   F   *   G   A

Answers

Answers to all these exercises can be found at **www.hybrid publications.com**

In this exercise, write out the melody shown in the top stave an octave lower in the bottom stave. Be warned – you will have to use ledger lines!

Listen to **Audio track 21** to hear what both versions of this melody sound like.

Audio track 21

Real life examples

You've already learned enough about music notation to understand many well known melodies. In this section we're going to give you notation for five tunes that you will recognise. To start with, try clapping out the rhythms, counting aloud as you do so.

Once you're confident that you've got the rhythm right try picking out the notes on a keyboard, or on your own instrument. Start slowly and steadily and gradually build up the speed.

Hopefully, you should recognise the tune in each case. Check that you've got it right by listening to the associated audio track for each example.

Example 1

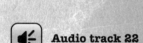

Example 2

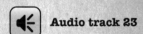

Example 3

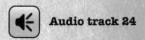

Here are a couple of longer examples. Although these are longer than any of the previous examples you've encountered, they both contain certain patterns of pitches and rhythms that are repeated.

When you come across these patterns you should find them easier to recognise and understand, so keep an eye out for them.

Example 4

Audio track 25

Example 5

Audio track 26

In each case, try singing or playing the notation yourself before checking the Audio tracks to hear full demonstrations of each exercise. Then follow the music along with the recording.

Listening examples

Now let's see if you can listen to some examples and write them down in music notation. Don't worry, we're going to start with some very simple rhythmic exercises. In each case the audio example will start with a four-beat count-in, so that you can judge the speed of the music. Then there will follow a four-bar example played on a snare drum. For each example, we'll tell you what type of note values are used – all you have to do is write them down!

Here's the first one. This uses only minims and quavers and doesn't include any rests:

 Audio track 27

 Answers

Answers to these exercises can be found at **www.hybrid publications.com**

Listen to the audio example as many times as you like and count out loud as you do so. Try to notice exactly where each note falls in relation to the counts of the bar.

Here's another example; this one uses only crotchets and quavers, and doesn't include any rests:

 Audio track 28

And finally, here's an exercise that uses crotchets and quavers and crotchet rests:

Audio track 29

Now let's try something similar with pitch. For each of these exercises we'll give you the starting note – all you need to do is listen to the Audio Examples and try to write down the notes that follow. To make the job a bit easier the notes will all be semibreves and they will only go up or down by one letter name at a time. (Oh, and there are no sharps or flats to worry about.)

Answers

Answers to all these exercises can be found at **www.hybrid publications.com**

Here's the first exercise, which contains three notes; listen really carefully and try to hear whether each note is higher or lower than the one before it:

Audio track 30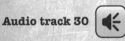

Now try this four-note sequence:

Audio track 31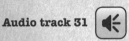

And finally, here's a six-note sequence:

Audio track 32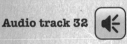

Listening to music and writing down the music notation is known as *transcription*. It's a really useful skill to develop as a musician because it will allow you to write down your own musical ideas, and to capture them in a permanent form. It will also allow you to listen to music you like and notate it. It can be tricky to get the hang of transcription – the more you use music notation the easier it will get, so do persevere.

Hints and tips for learning

When you start out learning to read music there are an awful lot of things to remember: note names, note values, different shaped rests, various rules and regulations and so on. Over the years people have developed all sorts of strategies for memorising these different facts and we present a selection below.

In fact, the best way to ensure that you can remember where notes go on the stave, for example, is to make up your own mnemonic. The very fact that you've made it up yourself will make it easier to remember – and the sillier it is the more memorable it will be.

Note names

The sensible way to remember note names is to use these two mnemonics (from the bottom of the stave going upwards):

Lines:	**E**very **G**ood **B**oy **D**eserves **F**igs
Spaces:	**F**-**A**-**C**-**E** (spells "face")

These mnemonics, while reliable, are not particularly memorable, so see if you can improve on them. Here are a couple of possible alternatives:

Lines:	**E**ating **G**reen **B**ananas **D**uring **F**ootball
Spaces:	**F**ighting **A**nts **C**atch **E**lephants

The possibilities are endless, so have some fun.

Note values

I'm afraid there's no easy way to learn the different note values. On the plus side, there are only five for you to learn, so it shouldn't be that difficult. As a general rule, the more tails or beams a note has the shorter it is likely to be; the larger and simpler the notehead the longer it lasts.

Just do it!

The single most helpful thing that you can do is to try to put all this theory into practice. Get hold of some sheet music and try to play or sing it. Find the music to one of your favourite recordings and try to follow it as you listen.

Rest values

The same goes for rest values, really. Again, the simpler the shape of the rest the longer it lasts; the more complex the shape the shorter the rest.

So a semibreve rest is a simple filled in rectangle, where as a semiquaver rest is a more complex shape. See page 7 for hints and tips on distinguishing between the semibreve rest (which hangs from the line) and the minim rest (which sits on the line).

Accidentals

Some people find it difficult to remember which symbol is a sharp and which is a flat. If you're have this problem then imagine a huge inflatable letter "b". Now imagine that someone has let some of the air out of this inflatable letter and allowed it to go slightly "flat"; hey presto, that's the shape of the flat sign: ♭.

The sharp sign (#), by contrast has lots of pointy edges and could in theory at least, puncture an enormous inflatable letter "b" (because it's sharp). Once you've got the flat sign and the sharp sign sorted, then the natural sign is easy.

If you're having difficulty remembering which sign means "up a semitone" and which means "down a semitone", again you can just think of the inflatable flat sign being gradually let "down".

General hints

In general, in the early stages of learning to read music it's much better to a little bit of study every day, if you can manage it. Far better to do 10 minutes, six days a week than to cram in an hour's work only once a week. Try to build a quarter of an hour into your daily schedule to devote to studying, whether it's reading another chapter of this book, doing some exercise sheets or testing yourself. You'll be amazed how quickly you see to see progress, and once you start to see results your motivation will go through the roof.

Game theory

Why not try to create your own musical games using the symbols and signs that you've learned. Create flash cards for each symbols and play with your friends and family.

Assignments

There's no worksheet for this chapter, as no new concepts have been introduced. Instead here are some ideas for assignments you might like to set yourself. They are designed to put your new-found musicals skills to the test in real-life practical applications.

Write down your own tune

Try writing your own short melody. It need only be four or five notes long, but you should be able to sing it back, or play it on your instrument, if you have one. Once you're happy with the melody, try to write it down in notation, using the symbols that you've learned so far. Then give the notation to a friend who can read music and see if they can play it back.

Find some sheet music

Why not visit your local music shop (or go online to **www.sheetmusicdirect.com**) and see if they have got sheet music for one of your favourite pieces or songs? You may be surprised at the range of material that's available – you'll find everything from Bach and Mozart through to the latest pop acts and guitar bands.

Once you've got some sheet music in front of you, listen to a recording of the piece and try to follow the music as you do so. Look out for all the signs and symbols that we've covered so far. You'll probably find quite a few bits of notation that we haven't covered so far, but don't worry about that at this stage.

Talk to other musicians

If you have friends or family who know how to read music, talk to them about how they learned. They may well be able to offer you some hints and tips, and if you get stuck they'll probably be able to help out.

All musicians have had to go through this process and most will be only too happy to help out another student.

Chapter 6:
Dots & Ties

Now it's time to take your understanding of rhythm on to the next level. In this chapter we'll introduce two powerful new symbols that will allow you to understand and use a huge variety of different rhythmic patterns.

Up to this point, you've used the five note values (semibreve, minim, crotchet, quaver and semiquaver) to create rhythms. But there are still some rhythms that you can't create using these note values. For example, if you wanted to play a note that lasted for three beats, how would you do it?

You have the semibreve, which lasts for four beats, and the minim, which lasts for two beats, but nothing inbetween. The closest you could get would be to play a minim for two beats followed by a crotchet, for one beat, like this:

In total, this rhythm lasts for the right number of beats, but it contains two notes, not one. But supposing we could join these two notes together somehow to form one single note of three beats?

That's exactly what we can do with a special musical symbol called a *tie*, like this:

The tie is the curved line joining the minim to the crotchet – it tells us to play one note that lasts for the duration of the two notes that are joined, or *tied*, together.

How to tie

When two notes are tied together we only play the first note, not the second one. The value of the second note is just added to the first note. Note that you can only tie together notes of the same pitch, for obvious reasons.

Rests & ties

Ties are only used with notes and not with rests. If we want to create a three-beat rest we can just put a two-beat rest next to a one-beat rest – there's no need to tie them together.

Answers

Answers to these exercises can be found at **www.hybrid publications.com**

And we're not limited to just tying two notes together – any number of note values can be tied together to produce an infinite variety of note lengths. For example, if we wanted to write down a note that lasts for three and a half beats, we could just add a tied quaver to the previous example:

Try the example below; in each case use combinations of note values that you already know and tie them together to form the total number of beats given below the stave. Then make up the rest of the beats in the bar with rests.

Now try the opposite: see if you can add up the following combinations of tied notes and figure out how long they last for:

Ties allow us to use a very limited number of note values to represent an almost infinite number of note durations – rather like the limited number of coins and notes in our currency allow us to make up many different amounts of money. They are a very powerful tool and an essential part of music notation.

In general, when tying notes together, the longest note value is given first, then the next longest and so on, ending with the shortest note value, although there are exceptions to this rule.

Introducing the dot

In fact, the tie is such a useful device that we find it all over the place in music notation. Just like the accidental, this can result in the written music becoming difficult to read, and, just as with accidentals, musicians have come up with a shorthand to reduce the amount of clutter on the page.

It turns out that by far the most common groups of tied notes that musicians need to use are those that represent odd multiples of other note values; for example, three crotchets, or three quavers, or three semiquavers. These are natural musical rhythms that crop up time and time again. With a system of ties we can represent these rhythms, of course, as minim-tied-to-crotchet, crotchet-tied-to-quaver and quaver-tied-to-semiquaver, respectively. But people writing down music soon got tired of writing these same configurations over and over again.

They came up with a simple shorthand to indicate that a note value should be increased by 50% – the dot. In the example below the first bar shows the tied version and the second bar shows the shorthand:

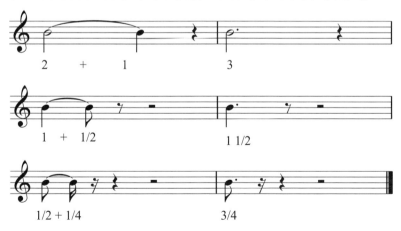

Or to put it another way:

dotted minim   =   minim + 50% of its length =   minim + crotchet
dotted crotchet =   crotchet + 50% of its length =   crotchet + quaver
dotted quaver =   quaver + 50% of its length =   quaver + semiquaver

Online material

Visit **www.hybrid publications.com** to watch a video showing how tied notes can be converted into dotted notes.

Keep it tidy

One advantage of the dot is that it is nice and small and doesn't get in the way of other bits of notation. Ties can take up a lot of valuable space on the page and tend to crash until other notes and rests.

Online material

Visit **www.hybrid publications.com** for a complete reference guide to dotted notes.

Rests and dots

Although we don't use ties with rests, we do use dots. So a dotted minim rest last for three beats, a dotted crotchet rest lasts for one and a half beats and so on. Again, this is simply for neatness on the page – the less black ink that is used the better!

Let's look at some common dotted note rhythms that crop up again and again in music notation. Try clapping each example while counting out loud. Then listen to **Audio track 33** which demonstrates all three dotted rhythms:

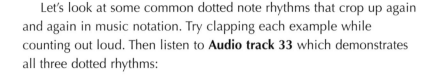

Note that there are two dotted rhythms that we haven't covered. Dotted semiquavers are used but are quite rare. Dotted semibreves on the other hand, being six (four + two) beats long, are too long to fit into a four-beat bar, and are therefore not found in this time signature.

Double dotted notes

Space doesn't allow for a full explanation here, but it is possible to take a dotted note and dot it again to further extend its duration. These are known as *double dotted* notes.

In these cases the second dot adds 50% of the value added by the first dot. So, in the case of a double dotted minim, the first dot adds one beat (50% of two beats) and the second dot adds half a beat (50% of the one beat added by the first dot) giving a total duration of three and a half beats.

Online material

Find out more about double dotted notes at **www.hybrid publications.com**

Audio track 33

Ties and barlines

So far, all the rhythmic examples we've looked at have fitted neatly into single bars. That is to say, none of the note durations have lasted longer than a bar or have crossed over from one bar to another.

So, supposing we wanted to place a four-beat note on beat three of a bar, how would we notate it? We can't place a semibreve on beat three, because this would mean having six beats in a four-beat bar. The solution is to use a tie to tie two minims across the barline, like this:

The two beats of the minim in bar 1 are added to the two beats of the minim in bar two, giving us the four-beat note that we wanted.

This technique can be extended indefinitely to produce notes that span multiple bars. For example, if we wanted to write a long note that lasted for four bars, we could just tie together four semibreves:

Dots vs. ties

So, why use dots sometimes and ties at other times, when they both do basically the same thing? Ties are much more versatile than dots as they can join together any number of different note values to create new note durations. Dots are simply a convenient way of notating very common rhythms that crop up all the time. It may seem confusing, but it works!

Let's work on some rhythms including both dots and ties. In the example below add notes of the duration shown below the stave. You'll need to use both dots and ties to get the correct number of beats in each bar:

Here's another similar exercise:

Now let's do the reverse. Write down the duration of each note below the stave and then clap the rhythm while counting out loud. Listen to **Audio track 34** to see if you got it right.

This example is demonstrated on **Audio track 35**:

You should find that you start to recognise certain combinations of dotted and undotted notes and that these rhythms gradually become embedded in your brain. Eventually you'll start to read groups of notes rather than individual note values – a bit like reading whole words instead of spelling them out letter-by-letter.

Syncopation

You now have all the techniques you need to write really quite complex rhythmic patterns in music notation. The dot and tie are powerful tools that allow us to represent complicated timelines of musical events.

Up to this point we've spent a lot of time talking about the beat, and we've measured all the rhythms that you've learned against it. Here's an example of a simple bar of quavers:

> **On or off**
>
> Musicians sometimes talk about *on-beats* and *off-beats*. On-beats are just the main beats of the bar that we count 1-2-3-4, while off beats are the subdivisions that fall between them, which we count by adding an "and": 1-&-2-&-3-&-4-&-

Some of these quavers coincide with the main beats of the bar, as written under the stave, and we describe these notes as being "on the beat". The other quavers fall on the "ands" inbetween the beats, and we describe these as being "off the beat".

As we've already discovered, notes falling "on the beat" are very important in music, and the first beat of the bar is generally the most important of all, as it marks out where the bar begins. However, it turns out that placing notes on the "off-beats" of the bar can produce some interesting rhythmic effects. Because the "rhythmic grid" of beats is so strong, and we perceive it so keenly when we listen to music, musicians and composers can make rhythms more interesting by deliberately putting important notes *off* the beat, so that they conflict with the underlying rhythmic grid.

This is a musical technique called *syncopation*. It's used in all genres of music, but in the twentieth century it was particularly associated with jazz, then other forms of popular music like rock'n'roll, dance music and hip hop. Syncopated rhythms are great fun to listen to, and to play, and they can be represented quite simply in music notation using the symbols and techniques you've already learned.

Let's start by clapping out this simple rhythm:

Notice how the quaver rests fall on the "on-beats" and the quaver notes fall on the off-beats. Count carefully and make sure you place the notes correctly on the "ands". Listen to **Audio track 36** to make sure that you've got it right.

This is an example of a syncopated rhythm – we have avoided the main beats of the bar and deliberately placed the notes of the rhythm on the off beats. Let's go one step further and make each of our quaver notes twice as long so that they actually cut across the beats of the bar:

Notice how each quaver has been tied across the beat to another quaver. In effect, the rhythm consists of a group of crotchets which, instead of beginning on the beat, have been displaced by a quaver and now begin on an off-beat. Try tapping out the beat with your foot and singing or playing the melody; once you get the hang of it, it's quite easy to do, and extremely satisfying.

Here's another syncopated rhythm for you to try. Listen to **Audio track 37** and follow the notation, counting aloud:

More fun with syncopation

Music without syncopated rhythms can feel a bit "square", with all the rhythms falling predictably on the beat. So composers and writers use all sorts of rhythmic tricks to try to keep the listener's interest.

One classic rhythmic trick is to take a simple rhythm and gradually displace it so that it appears in different parts of the bar, and on different beats. As listeners, we like this because we recognise the basic rhythm and can latch on to it; however, because it constantly appears in different positions in the bar, it always sounds a bit different and we never get bored of it.

Here's an example of this trick in action. In this example the rhythm starts on beat one of bar 2. However, it soon starts appearing on different beats of the bar! Count carefully and have a go at clapping out this rhythm:

If you have access to a piano, try playing the melody, or sing it. Then compare with the recording on **Audio track 38**. See how catchy the melody is, because of its intruiging rhythmic pattern.

Why not try yourself? On the stave below we've written out a simple melody that lasts for three beats. Try writing it out again, immediately afterwards, so that it starts on beat four of bar 1. Then add another repeat starting on beat three of bar 2. Finally add the same rhythm a fourth time, to fill up the four bars. Try singing the melody back; compare it to **Audio track 39** to see how it should sound.

The push

We're going to move on to talk about one particular type of syncopation, which is very common in all types of popular music

As music has developed over the years, composers and writers and become adept at figuring out what listeners expect from a piece of music. And equally, listeners have become very good at understanding what a piece of music is likely to do – if we are familiar with a genre of music, then a lot of the time we have an idea in our heads of what the music is likely to do next.

As listeners we like a bit of predictability – but not too much, otherwise the music will become boring. So composers are constantly trying to surprise us by breaking music rules or doing something out of the ordinary. And what could be more predictable than the first beat of the bar? In nearly every example we've looked at in this book so far, the first beat of the bar as been the most important. Lots of melodies and rhythmic patterns start on the first beat of the bar and we like to know where it is.

So what would happen if we deliberately avoided the first beat of the bar? Take a look at the melody below:

You should notice immediately that none of the notes in this melody fall on the first beat of the bar. In each bar, there is a quaver on the last half-beat of the bar, which it tied across the barline.

This is a specific type of syncopation, called a *push*, and it's found in most types of popular music, from jazz through to pop music, R'n'B and rock. The push serves two purposes: firstly, it takes away the predictability of the first beat of the bar, and secondly, it adds a sense of movement, because key notes are always arriving slightly early.

The unexpected

Music is often about creating expectations in the listener and then either fulfilling or denying those expectations. We expect important notes to appear on the first beat of the bar, because we've heard it so many times; paradoxically, we then enjoy it when this expectation is not fulfilled!

In effect, the push moves the starting point of the rhythmic pattern back by half a beat, to start on beat four and a half. When written down the push is immediately recognisable – just look out for a quaver tied across the barline. Here's another example:

 Audio track 40

Listen to **Audio track 40** to hear what this sounds like. Notice that the note on beat four and half is accented, just as it would be if it were on the first beat of the bar.

 Top tip

A quaver tied across the barline, is a sure-fire sign of the push, so look out for it.

Pushing further

Beat one is the most important beat of the bar, so that's where we get the biggest effect from a push. The second most important beat of the bar is beat three, and we can therefore also get an interesting rhythmic effect by adding a push that cuts across beat three, like this:

Audio track 41

In this example, we've kept the push before beat one, but have added a new push before beat three; look out for the quaver on beat two and a half, tied across beat three. Listen to **Audio track 41** to hear how this sounds.

You might think that the ultimate syncopation would be to move every note in the bar so that it falls on an off-beat. Strangely enough, this doesn't really work – we need to hear some notes falling on the beat to remind our ears where the beat is. Otherwise we mentally revise our perception of the beat by half a beat and start hearing all the off-beat notes as on-beat notes!

Worksheet 6 (answers on page 164)

1. Simplify this rhythm using dots:

2. Add notes to the stave according to the numbers of beats given below the stave. This will require you to use both dots and ties:

3	3		1 1/2	1 1/2	3

3. Fill in the missing cells in this table. We've done the first one for you:

1X	o.	=	12X	♪
2X	♩.	=		♪
12X	♪	=		♩.
4X	♩.	=		o
3X	♪	=		♩.

4. Write the number of beats belonging to each note under the stave:

Chapter 7:
Time & Key

In this chapter we're going to introduce two new concepts that extend the way in which we can use rhythm and pitch. We've seen how important the concepts of beats and bars are to music; they provide the rhythmic grid against which all the other elements of music can be placed. Every example we've looked at so far has had four beats in each bar. The chances are that if you hear a piece of music on the radio or play a favourite tune, it will also have four beats per bar. We call this property of a piece of music its *meter*.

However, there is no reason why music *has* to have four beats per bar. Admittedly, an awful lot of music does – four beats per bar is by far and away the most common meter, particularly in popular music. However, there's plenty of music out there with three, five, six or even seven beats in a bar. So, how do we go about representing these meters in music notation?

Time signatures

You'll remember that the number four at the beginning of the stave tells us that there are four beats in each bar. It's called the *time signature* and it describes the meter of the piece of music:

The time signature tells us that every bar in this piece will contain four beats. So, let's suppose that we want to write down a melody that has three beats per bar – all we have to do is change the time signature from four to three, like this:

Audio track 42

Audio track 43

Waltz time

Pieces with three beats in a bar are sometimes referred to as being in *waltz* time. Historically, many musical forms were developed for people to dance to (just as they are today) and the waltz is a ballroom dance that is specifically designed to be danced to pieces with three beats in the bar. Once again, the first beat of the bar is the most important, with beats two and three being less important.

Here are another couple of examples of melodies in waltz time:

Listen to **Audio track 42** to hear how this sounds. Note the difference that changing the time signature makes to the feel of the music; it has a bouncy yet flowing rhythm. Here's another example:

This example is demonstrated on **Audio track 43**. Practise counting along and notice how the first beat of each bar is accented, with beats two and three being much lighter.

All the other rules you know about rhythm (note values, dots, ties etc.) still apply in waltz time – the only difference is that we have three beats in the bar instead of four. Of course, this means that there is no room for the semibreve, with its four beat value, but all the other note values that you've used so far can be used in exactly the same way.

Let's talk units

So, we've seen how we can change the time signature to indicate how many beats there are in each bar. On the previous page we changed it to three to create waltz time, but we could have changed it to five, six or seven and created perfectly viable pieces of music. But there's one other piece of information that we've been giving every time we've defined the meter of a piece of music. We've always said "This piece has three (or four, or five) *beats* per bar". In other words, we've used the beat as a unit with which to measure time. This makes sense, of course, because the beat is a fundamental unit of music. We all know what we mean when we say one beat, don't we? Well, maybe not – take a look at the example below:

Take five!

Pieces with five beats in the bar are quite unusual. The most famous is 'Take Five' by the jazz composer and performer Dave Brubeck. Try to find a recording of this piece and try counting along with it – it's surprisingly easy!

Take a listen to **Audio track 44** and follow the music notation, counting out loud as you do so. This is quite a fast piece so the beats go by pretty quickly. Now try counting like this – instead of counting quickly from 1–4 in each bar, count at half the speed from 1–2:

Online material

If you want to find out more about strange meters, then visit **www.hybrid publications.com** to find suggested listening.

It's actually more comfortable to count this piece of music in two than it is to count it in four. But if we change the way we count it we have to change the way it's written, because all of our note values are based around numbers of beats.

Audio track 44

This confusion arises because we haven't specified the *units* that we are counting in. As we've seen, the piece on page 85 could be counted in two or four; if we want to remove any possible ambiguity the notation has to tell us both the number of beats in each bar, and the value of each beat.

Measuring the beat

So, to define the meter of a piece we need to give two pieces of information, like this: "This piece has four crotchets per bar". This tells us how many beats to count in each bar and what note value each of those beats represents. We could just write "This piece has four crotchets per bar" at the top of our piece of music, but as with most aspects of music notation, a shorthand method has developed over the years.

In order to understand this shorthand method let's revisit our five major note values, the semibreve, minim, crotchet, quaver and semiquaver:

𝅝	=	4 beats
𝅗𝅥	=	2 beats
♩	=	1 beat
♪	=	1/2 beat
𝅘𝅥𝅮	=	1/4 beat

Up to this point we've defined each of these note values in terms of the number of beats that they receive: the semibreve is worth four beats, the minim is worth two beats, and so on.

However, in this instance, that's not a particularly helpful way of thinking about it, because, after all, the beat is the very thing that we are trying to define. So, we have to come up with a different way of describing each of these note values.

Downbeats

For every time signature, there is a specific way for a conductor to beat time. For example, for a waltz, the conductor will outline the shape of a triangle, with the first beat of the bar being indicated by a downward motion. It is for this reason that the first beat of the bar is sometimes referred to as the *downbeat*.

We started out back on page 7 with one note value, the semibreve. So why not define all the other note values in terms of their relationship to the semibreve – after all, that's how we created them in the first place, by dividing the semibreve in half and half again.

So, let's ask ourselves how many times each note value would fit into a semibreve. Firstly, the minim; the semibreve is worth four beats and the minim is worth two, so we could fit two minims into the time of one semibreve. Similarly, the crotchet is worth one beat, so we could fit four crotchets into the time of one semibreve.

If we continue, we end up with a table that looks like this:

𝅝	fits into a 𝅝	1 time
𝅗𝅥	fits into a 𝅝	2 times
♩	fits into a 𝅝	4 times
♪	fits into a 𝅝	8 times
𝅘𝅥𝅯	fits into a 𝅝	16 times

Upbeats

Similarly on the last beat of the bar, the conductor's baton moves upward to start the pattern again, and this beat of the bar has become known as the upbeat.

So now all that remains is for us to put together our two key pieces of information:
1. Number of beats in the bar
2. Value of each beat

If we wanted to represent a piece with 4 crotchet beats per bar, these two values would be:
1. 4 (beats per bar)
2. 4 (because a semibreve contains four crotchets)

And this is exactly how we write the full time signature:

Different time signatures

So, instead of using one figure at the beginning of each piece to signify the meter, we will now use two. Our familiar four crotchet beats per bar will be represented like this:

While the three crochets per bar, waltz time, would be represented like this:

And that's not all we can do – here's how we would represent a piece in three, counting in minims:

Or how about a piece in 4, counting in quavers:

You can see that this system gives us complete control over the meter of the music – and remember that we don't have to restrict ourselves to three or four beats per bar, we can have anything from two beats per bar upwards.

Here are some exercises to help you get to grips with time signatures. Let's start by looking at a piece in 3/4. In each bar, add rests to make the total number of crotchet beats add up to three:

Top tip

Remember that the bottom number of the time signature tells you the type of beats in the bar, and the top number tells you how many of them there are.

And now do the same thing for this piece in 3/2 – this time there are three minim beats per bar:

Answers

Answers to all these exercises can be found at **www.hybrid publications.com**

Here are two examples where the time signature has been missed out. Count up the beats in each bar, and insert the correct time signature:

Hint: these two examples use time signatures that we haven't come across before. Don't worry, just add up the total number of beats in each bar, and the type of each beat, and you'll be able to figure out the correct time signature.

Don't forget that there are extra worksheets and exercises available to download from **www.hybridpublications.com**.

Back to accidentals

Let's leave the world of rhythm for the time being and return to the subject of Chapter 4: accidentals. As you'll remember, we introduced three symbols, the sharp, the flat, and the natural, which can be used to alter pitches upwards or downwards by a semitone.

As a quick refresher, here are some notes on the stave that use accidentals, with the corresponding notes on the piano keyboard:

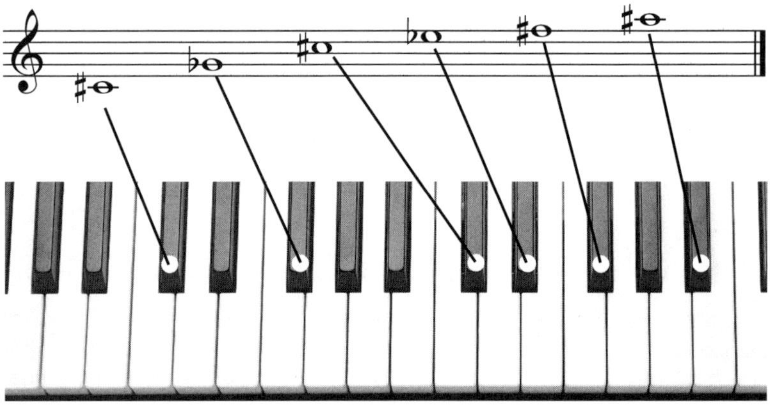

Quick tip

Sharp
Up a semitone
Flat
Down a semitone
Natural
Cancels sharp or flat
Remember that accidentals only last a bar.

And here's a sample piece of music using sharps. Remember that an accidental lasts for a whole bar, so notes of the same pitch that are repeated later in the same bar are automatically also affected by any accidentals earlier in the bar:

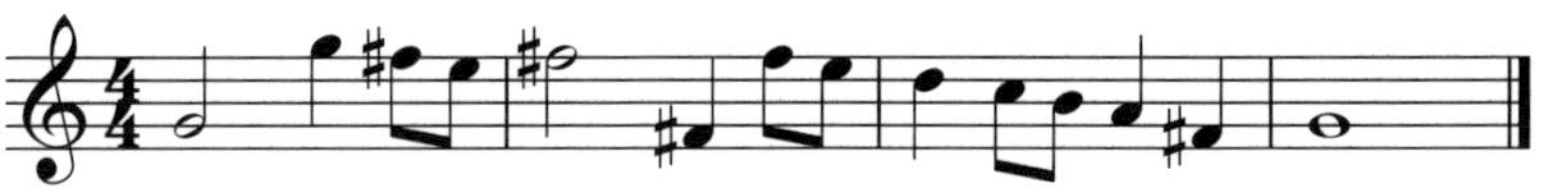

In bar two, the first F of the bar is sharpened, and this sharp also affects the second F in the bar, even though that note doesn't have a sharp sign in front of it. In fact, if you look closely at this piece you'll notice that every single F in the piece is sharpened. (Remember to check the F on the top line of the stave and the F in the bottom space.) Because of the way that music is organised, this is quite common.

As we've seen several times before, musicians are a pretty lazy bunch – we don't like to make any task any more difficult or time-consuming than it needs to be. So, if every F in a piece needs to be played as an F sharp, surely all we need to do is to put a global instruction at the top of the piece to say exactly that: "Every time you see an F in this piece, play it as an F sharp".

And that's exactly what we do, with a device called a *key signature*. If we add an sharp symbol on the F line, right after the clef, that acts as an instruction to the musician to let him or her know that every single F in the piece should actually be played as an F sharp.

Top tip

Unlike accidentals, the key signature tells you that *every* single note of that letter name, in *every* octave should be either sharpened or flattened.

This instruction applies to every single F, no matter what octave it is in. So, the Fs that appear in the bottom space of the stave will all be sharpened, as well as those that occur on the top line.

Try for yourself – here's a piece written out in full, with every F sharp marked:

Answers

Answers to all these exercises can be found at **www.hybrid publications.com**

Now write out the melody again, but this time use a key signature:

Imagine how much time this saves if you're writing out a long piece of music that might have hundreds of F sharps in it!

Key signatures are a very neat way to notate accidentals, but what happens if we have a piece with F sharps all the way through, until the last bar, where we find an unsharpened F?

Well, we can still use a key signature of F sharp – all we have to do is to insert a natural sign in front of the F that we don't want to sharpen. This overrules the key signature and tells the musician to play the unsharpened note:

In fact, we can use any number of naturals to cancel out the key signature, although, of course, if you end up using more naturals than sharps then you'd be better off taking the key signature out and using individual sharp signs!

What do key signatures mean?

Well, we know what they mean – they tell us to sharpen one particular note every time it occurs. That's true, but there's a little more to it than that. It turns out that in Western music, certain patterns of sharps and flats tend to crop up time and time again. For example, you might find some pieces where virtually every F and C are sharpened, or you might find another piece where nearly every B and E are flattened. The reason for this is that most types of music are based around certain common collections of notes (these are called *scales* and we'll deal with them in Chapter 10). A piece based on one of these collections of notes is said to be in that *key*.

As it happens, the number of sharps or flats in these collections of notes is enough to identify them uniquely. The practical upshot of this is that the *key signature,* on its own, is enough to tell us what key a piece of music is in. This turns out to be a very useful piece of information, and explains the term *key signature* – like the time signature it tells us a unique and important property of the piece.

Here are the first few most common key signatures. Although a key signature can have up to seven sharps or flats, for the time being we'll concentrate only on the first three of each type. Here are the first three sharp key signatures:

And here are the first three flat key signatures:

There are a couple of things to notice straight away:

1. Key signatures never mix sharps and flats
2. Key signatures build up incrementally – the first sharp key signature has F sharp, the second has F sharp and C sharp, the third and F sharp, C sharp and G sharp, and so on. To put it another way, each new key signature adds one more accidental to the one that preceded it.

Look a little more closely and you might notice that there is a pattern in the way the sharps and flats in the key signatures are laid out. Starting from the first sharp, F, we move up five letter names to get to the next sharp, C (F, G, A, B, C), and we then move up another five to get to the next sharp, G (C, D, E, F, G).

In the flat key signatures, we move up four letter names from the first flat, B, to the second, E (B, C, D, E) and another four to get to the third, A (E, F, G, A). Or to think of it another way, you go down five letter names to create each new flat. As we'll see later on , these patterns hold true for all keys signatures, right up to seven sharps or flats.

Online material

Visit **www.hybrid publications.com** for a complete reference guide to key signatures.

Worksheet 7 (answers on page 165)

1. Add the correct time signature to this example:

2. Add the correct time signature to this example:

3. Add the correct time signature to this example:

4. Write out this example again, using a key signature to remove the accidentals:

5. Write out the correct pattern of sharps or flats for these key signatures:

1 flat   *2 sharps*   *3 flats*   *3 sharps*

Answers

Answers to this worksheet can be found on page 165.

Online material

Additional worksheets are available at **www.hybrid publications.com**.

Online material

Visit **www.hybrid publications.com** for an interactive pitch & rhythm test.

Chapter 8: Navigation

Let's take a break from key signatures for a while to think about another vital area of music notation – finding your way around. Most of the musical examples we've looked at in this book so far have been about four bars long, and have probably lasted about ten seconds.

Yet we know that most pieces of music are much longer than that: the average pop song is around three minutes, a symphony can last well over an hour and some operas go on for several days! When these longer pieces are written down they can take up hundreds of pages of sheet music. In the early days of music notation all of this had to be written out by hand, which was an extremely laborious and time-consuming operation. So there was a powerful incentive for musicians to come up with more concise ways of representing music.

Many of these devices take advantage of the fact that music includes a lot of repetition. Sometimes people use the word "repetitive" as a derogatory term to describe music that is uninventive or boring, but in actual fact all music is repetitive. In fact, repetition is a key ingredient of all good music. As listeners we enjoy hearing repeated musical material; it's something that our ears recognise and feels like familiar territory. (As with all things, you can have too much repetition, of course, but some repetition is integral to all music around the world.)

Having said all the above, it will come as no surprise to discover that the first labour-saving device that we're going to look at is called the *repeat mark*. Look at the example below:

Note that the final barline of this example has changed. There are now two vertical lines, one thin, and one thick, and there are two small dots in the second and third spaces of the stave.

Techno-tip

"Setting" or "engraving" music is a highly skilled operation and used to take years of training. These days music notation is all set by computer, using powerful notation programs like *Sibelius* and *Finale*.

This symbol is a repeat mark and it carries a simple instruction for musicians: "Go back to the first repeat mark you find facing the other way and start playing the music from that point." So let's add a repeat mark facing the other way:

Audio track 45

 Repeat tip

If a repeat mark appears right at the beginning of a piece it can be missed out. After all, where else can you go back to that is earlier than the beginning of the piece?

So to play this example correctly we play the four bars until we reach the repeat mark at the end; this tells us to go back to the beginning and play the four bars again. Listen to **Audio track 45** to hear how this sounds.

Repeat marks nearly always appear in pairs; a left-facing repeat (or end repeat mark) and a right-facing repeat (or start repeat) and, unless marked otherwise, are only active once. So, the second time you come to the end repeat mark you ignore it and move directly on to the next bar. Here's another example featuring repeat marks:

 Audio track 46

In this case, play the first four bars until you reach the end repeat mark; then go back to the start repeat mark in bar 3 and play the last two bars again. Listen to **Audio track 46** to hear how this should sound.

Although most repeat marks only work for one repeat, as mentioned above, sometime the words "Play three times" are added to indicate the number of times that the repeat should be played:

Play three times

Different endings

One slight variation on the basic repeat structure is needed to cover repeated sections that differ slightly in the final bar. Take a look at this example:

Audio track 47

Notice that the last two bars have brackets over them, containing the numbers 1 and 2 – these are known as the *1st* and *2nd time bars*. These brackets tells us to play the 1st time bar on the 1st time through and the 2nd time bar on the 2nd time through.

Play it again

We're not limited to just 1st and 2nd time bars, we can have 3rd, 4th and 5th time bars if we want.

Here's how to interpret this structure:
1. Play the first four bars, including the 1st time bar, until you reach the end repeat mark
2. Return to the opening repeat mark
3. Play the first three bars again, as before
4. This time, ignore the 1st time bar and skip on to the 2nd time bar
Listen to **Audio track 47** to hear how this should sound.

Here's another repeat structure featuring 1st and 2nd time bars. This time the music goes onto two lines. When you get to the end of the first stave , just move down to the stave below, again reading from left to right. **Audio track 48** demonstrates what this example sounds like – listen and follow the music:

Audio track 48

Back to the beginning

Occasionally you may come across the instruction "D.C." at the end of a piece. This abbreviation stands for the Italian term "Da Capo". "Capo" means "head" in Italian, so this indication is telling us to go back to the head of the piece – in other words, go back to the start.

The D.C. indication is most often seen in conjunction with the words "al Fine", meaning until the end. So the phrase "D.C al Fine" means, "Go back to the beginning and continue playing until you reach the end". But how do you know when you've reached the end? Very simple really, just look out for the word "Fine" appearing above the stave – this marks the point where you should stop. Here's an example of the "D.C. al Fine" structure:

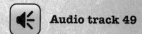
Audio track 49

Phew!

Once you've read this explanation of how to interpret the "D.C. al Fine" structure, you'll understand why we abbreviate it to just "D.C. al Fine".

Here's how to interpret this structure: play through the 1st and 2nd time bars as before. After the 2nd time bar, continue through the next six bars until you get to the end of the example, where you'll find the "D.C. al Fine" indication. Then return back to the beginning of the music and play through again, playing the repeat as before (going to the 1st time bar, then back the beginning again), until you finally reach the 2nd time bar for the second time, where you'll find the "Fine" indication. Follow through with **Audio track 49** to see how it all works.

Look out for the sign

A common modification to the "D. C. al Fine" structure is the "D.S. al Fine", which is short for "Dal Segno al Fine". Again, this is an Italian phrase meaning "Go back to the sign until the end". Instead of returning to the beginning of the piece, as with the D. C., in this structure you return to the point at which the "segno" or sign appears. The segno is a squiggly S symbol that looks like this: 𝄋. Here's an example of the "D. S. al Fine" structure:

Jargon buster 💡

D. C.
Go back to the beginning
D. S.
Go back to the sign (segno)
Fine
The end

Audio track 50 🔊

This structure is interpreted in exactly the same way as the "D. C. al Fine" structure on the previous page, the only difference being that you return to the segno and not right back to the beginning. Listen to **Audio track 50** and follow the music to see how it works. Notice how all these structures allow longer pieces of music to be represented in the most concise way possible. Using repeat marks, D.C. and D.S. markings, we can avoid writing out repeated sections of music again. This not only saves time, but actually makes it easier to memorise pieces of music.

The tail

Coda literally means "tail" in Italian and so the Coda is a small piece of music that is tacked on at the end, in the same way as a tail is pinned onto a donkey in the children's game.

Audio track 51

The Coda

A common variation on the "D.C./D.S. al Fine" structure is known as the "D.C./D.S. al Coda". In this case the D.C. and D.S. indications are used as before to return either to the beginning of the piece or to the segno. However, instead of then continuing to the "Fine" marking, in this structure, the reader follows the music until a "To Coda" marking is introduced. At this point, you jump to the Coda section and continue until the end of the piece.

Here's an example of a D.S al Coda structure:

Listen to **Audio track 52** to hear this played through. Look out for the jump back to the segno and then for the jump to the Coda. The D.S. al Coda structure is probably the most commonly used navigation structure in written music, so it's worth familiarising yourself with it.

Double barlines

As we've seen already with the repeat mark, sometimes in music notation the barline is altered to represent particular structural features of the music. In addition to the repeat mark, there are a couple of other types of barlines that you should be aware of.

The double barline, as its name suggests, simply looks like two normal barlines close together:

Double barline

Top tip

Sections in music are sometimes labelled with letters to help musicians find their way around. The first section might be labelled A, the second section B and so on. In orchestral scores these "rehearsal letters" are used to save time when practising by allowing the musicians quickly to find a particular point in the music.

The double barline is generally used to indicate a transition point between two different sections of a piece of music or some other structural change. As such, it doesn't have any direct impact on what the musician is required to do; it is simply there to indicate the underlying structure of the piece of music, which can help a performer both to play and to memorise the music.

The other common type of altered barline is the final barline, which, again as its name suggests, is used at the end of a piece to indicate that there is no more music to follow. The final barline is also a double barline, but unlike the example above, the two lines are of different widths, with the second line being thicker than the first:

Final barline

In older sheet music the final barline is also accompanied by the word "Fine", but this is not strictly necessary.

Other types of barline that you might encounter include the dotted barline, which indicates editorial or optional divisions of the bar.

Worksheet 8 (answers on page 166)

1. Simplify this example using repeat marks:

2. Write out this example in full (without the repeat marks):

3. Match up the Italian terms with their correct translation:

D.S al Fine	Go back to the beginning
Coda	Go back to the beginning and then jump to the Coda
D.C	The "tail" – a short section at the end of a piece
D.C al Coda	Go back to the sign and continue until the end

4. Why is an opening repeat mark not needed at the beginning of a piece?

Chapter 9:
The Bass Clef

In this chapter we'll introduce a new technique for writing down pitches lower than those that we have previously notated. Before we do so, let's have a quick refresher on the notes that we have encountered so far:

Notice that we have used a ledger line below the stave to accommodate the note C, also known as Middle C. Let's do the same again, and add another two notes below middle C:

We can continue doing this indefinitely, to indicate lower and lower notes – here we've used three ledger lines to get down to the note F:

The only problem with this system is that, as more and more ledger lines are added, it becomes harder and harder to count the number of ledger lines and therefore to identify the pitch that is being notated. It is much easier to tell the different between two and three ledger lines than it is to tell the different between four or five. So if we want to represent pitches much lower then this F, we need a different system.

When we introduced the treble clef, back on page 17, we described it as a symbol that identifies one line on the stave and tells the musician which note it represents. The treble clef identifies the note G and tells us that it is represented by the second line of the stave (from the bottom):

This function is recognised in the treble clef's other name, the G clef.

So if we need to represent notes lower down the keyboard, why not just create a new clef that identifies a lower note and places it on a different stave? That's exactly what we do with the F clef, or bass clef:

Like the treble clef, the F clef curls around one line on the stave; in this case it's the fourth line from the bottom. As the name suggests, this clef identifies this line as representing the note F, which can be found here on the keyboard:

F

The F clef is more commonly known as the bass clef.

Clef names

The F clef's more common name, the bass clef, originates in the fact that it allows the range of the male bass voice to be written comfortably on it. You may recall that this is the same reason for the naming of the treble clef.

Having identified the note F, we can now place the other white notes on the stave, like this:

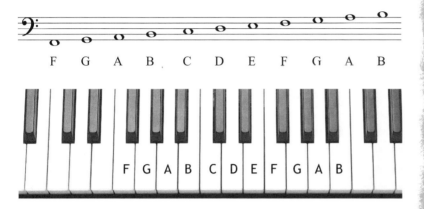

F   G   A   B   C   D   E   F   G   A   B

Other clefs

In fact, other voice types also have clefs specifically designed for them, such as the Alto and Tenor clefs. We won't be discussing these other clefs in this book as they are much less common than the treble and bass clefs.

By adding accidentals we can represent all the white and black notes in this range:

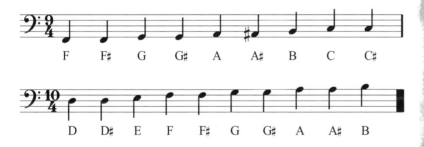

F   F♯   G   G♯   A   A♯   B   C   C♯

D   D♯   E   F   F♯   G   G♯   A   A♯   B

As with the treble clef there are various mnemonics which can help you to remember the names of the pitches that correspond to the lines and spaces of the stave. Here are a couple of suggestions, but feel free to invent your own (again, the more ridiculous the better):

Lines:	**G**ood **B**oys **D**eserve **F**ine **A**pples
Lines:	**G**oing **B**ananas **D**oing **F**unny **A**cronyms
Spaces:	**A**nts **C**an't **E**at **G**rass
Spaces:	**A**fter **C**oughing **E**at **G**rapes

Here's a page of exercises to help you get to grips with the bass clef and the names of the notes. Start by filling in the relevant notes to form two four-letter words:

B   E   A   D   F   A   D   E

This time we've given you the notes, all you have to do is fill in the letter names underneath the stave:

Answers

Answers to all these exercises can be found at **www.hybrid publications.com**

Just as on the treble clef, there are four letter names that appear twice on the stave. We've given you the two Fs on the stave below; can you find the other three pairs?

F   F

Online material

Test your knowledge of notes on the bass clef with the musical Sudoku puzzles at **www.hybrid publications.com**

Finally, notate these notes on the keyboard using the bass clef, using sharp signs where necessary:

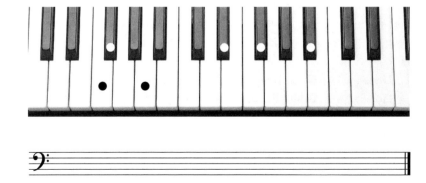

The bass clef and ledger lines

Just as with the treble clef, we can use ledger lines above and below the stave to extend the range of notes that we can represent. Adding lines below the stave, we can get down to two Cs below middle C, and further:

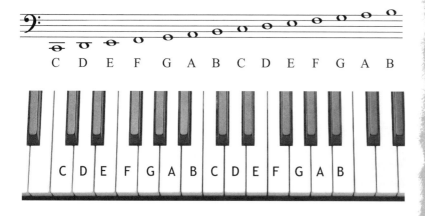

As we add ledger lines above the bass clef we start to cross over with the notes that we previously plotted on the treble clef:

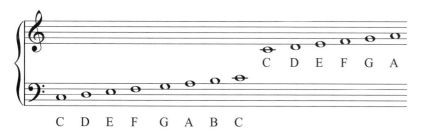

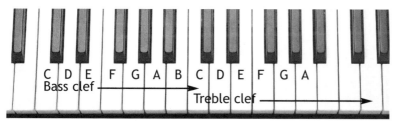

Notice how middle C sits in the middle, in between the two staves – another reason for its name.

Piano music

A two-stave layout using the treble clef for the top stave and the bass clef for the bottom stave is the standard format for presenting piano music. The treble stave is generally used for notes played by the right hand and the bass stave is usually used for notes played by the left hand.

Online material

Visit **www.hybrid publications.com** for a complete reference guide to note names across both the treble and bass staves.

Worksheet 9 (answers on page 167)

1. Write these notes on the stave below (remember that some note names appear in two places on the stave):

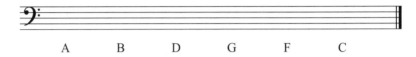

A   B   D   G   F   C

2. Write the letter names of these notes under the stave:

3. Add notes on the stave to spell these three-letter words:

E   G   G   A   D   D   B   A   G

4. Write down the letter names of these notes underneath the stave to form three more three-letter words:

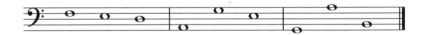

5. Write this example out an octave lower (you'll need to use ledger lines):

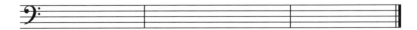

Chapter 10:
Keys & Scales

Back in Chapter 7, we introduced the idea that pieces of music are based around certain collections of notes. We discovered that by looking at the patterns of accidentals in each collection of notes we could describe a unique property of the piece of music, its *key*, which is identified by the *key signature*.

In this chapter we're going to explore these collections of notes, or *scales*, in more detail. The most important scale in Western classical music (and a lot of popular music too) is called the *major* scale. The name itself tells you that this collection of notes Is Important!

The major scale

Let's take a look at a major scale, beginning on C:

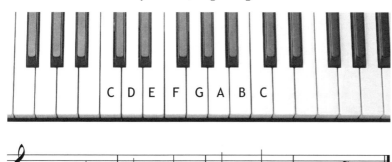

Have a listen to this scale on **Audio track 52**. To start with there are a few basic properties of this scale that we should note:

1. It spans an octave (i.e. it begins and ends on C). In theory it can be extended indefinitely above and below the octave we've shown above, but for the time being this is all we need to look at.

2. It contains seven notes before arriving back on C again. Scales don't have to contain seven notes, but lots of them do.

3. This particular scale contains only white notes, no black ones. This isn't true of all scales, as we'll see.

Audio track 52

109

So, what is it that makes the major scale such an important collection of notes? After all, in theory anyone could choose a collection of notes and base a piece of music around them – why these particular notes in this particular order?

The unique properties of this scale are not so much the notes themselves but the unique pattern of spaces *between those notes*. You'll remember that we measure the distance between notes in *semitone*s, so that C sharp, for example, is said to be *one semitone* above C:

Let's apply this system to the notes in our C major scale:

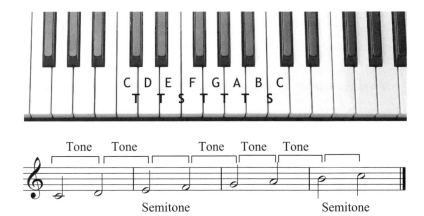

What we find is a pattern of one semitone and two semitone gaps between the notes of the scale. As we mentioned back in Chapter 4 two semitones are generally referred to as a *tone*, so we can describe this pattern as a sequence of *tones* and *semitones*. The crucial point is that this pattern is common to all major scales, not just the C major scale. Or, in other words, if we know the pattern that defines the major scale we can generate any major scale from its starting note.

Other scales

There are many other different types of scale apart from the major scale. You may have heard of the minor scale, for example. Other scales include the whole-tone scale, the pentatonic scale and the octatonic scale.

Tones and semitones

So, we've discovered a unique pattern underlying the major scale, which can be written like this:

Tone Tone Semitone Tone Tone Tone Semitone, or
TTSTTTS, for short

It is this underlying pattern that gives the major scale its character, and, as we'll see, it is also responsible for creating the key signatures that we encountered back in Chapter 7.

Let's start by applying this pattern to a new starting note. This time let's start on G: by applying the pattern we can deduce that the next note of the scale must be A (a tone away from G) and the next note must be B (a tone away from A). So far, so good:

Key fact

It is the position of the semitones in the major scale pattern that gives it its unique character. Note in particular that there is a semitone between the penultimate note of the scale and the last note. Our ear wants to hear this note "resolve" upwards to the key note of the scale, and this tension forms a vital part of the scale's character.

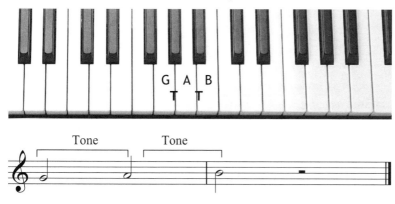

So we've had two tones, now we need a gap of a semitone, which takes us from B to C, followed by a tone, from C to D and another tone from D to E:

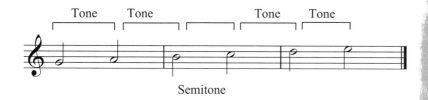

Finally, to complete the pattern of tones and semitones we need to add another tone and a semitone. Moving up a tone from E takes us to our first black note, F#, and then adding the final semitone brings us back to our starting note, G:

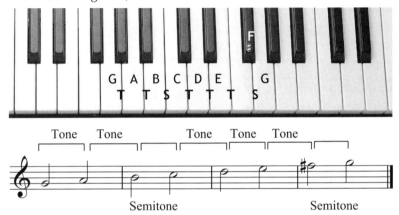

Audio track 53

Have a listen to **Audio track 53** to hear what the G major scale sounds like.

So, by using our underlying pattern of tones and semitones we've created a major scale starting on G, or a *G major scale*, as it is known. The important thing to notice here is that this pattern has forced us to include a black note, or accidental, for the first time. If we were to use this collection of notes to write a piece of music, every F in the piece would need to be played as F sharp. And in that situation we would use a key signature to simplify the notation. So, for example, the G major scale written out with a key signature would look like this:

Key fact

Note that in G major we have a key signature with an F sharp in it. Or to put it another way, if we look at the key signature and go up one letter name from the sharpened note, we get the key of the piece.

The scale of G major will always need a key signature of one sharp. Or to put it another way, the key signature of one sharp tells us that this example is in the *key of G major*. It turns out that this is one of the most important properties of a piece of music; G is the most important note in a piece in G major and the other notes are all related to it.

Let's try creating another major scale, this time, starting on D. We've done the first few notes for you – see if you can finish it off:

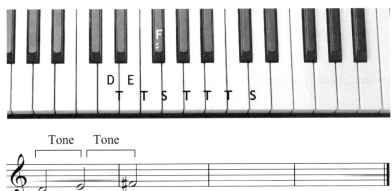

Key fact

The same thing applies with this example. If we look at the last sharp in the key signature, C sharp, and go up by one letter name, we get the key of the piece: D major.

Check **www.hybridpublications.com** for the correct answer to this exercise. You should find that the finished scale of D major contains two sharps, an F sharp and a C sharp, and therefore has a key signature of two sharps. Here's the scale written out again with its key signature:

Online material

Visit **www.hybrid publications.com** for more examples of how we can use this pattern to generate different major scales.

In the major scale, as we've seen, some notes are more important than others. Musicians have names for each of the notes of the scale, which describe their function and importance, like this:

1st note	=	tonic
2nd note	=	supertonic
3rd note	=	mediant
4th note	=	subdominant
5th note	=	dominant
6th note	=	submediant
7th note	=	leading note

Don't worry too much about these names; for the time being, just note that the 5th note of the scale is called the *dominant*; this is because, after the tonic, the dominant is the next most important.

Worksheet 10 (answers on page 168)

1. Mark the pattern of tones and semitones under this scale of D major:

2. Complete this major scale by using the pattern of tones and semitones to predict what the notes are:

3. Complete this major scale and then deduce the correct key signature:

4. Join up the notes of the scale in the left-hand column with their correct musical names in the right-hand column:

1	Supertonic
2	Subdominant
3	Tonic
4	Submediant
5	Mediant
6	Leading note
7	Dominant

Chapter 11: Intervals

The major scale is one of the cornerstones of Western music; its unique combination of tones and semitones creates many of the familiar features of melodies and harmonies that span hundreds of years of musical composition. It's clear from this that the distances between notes are pretty powerful – they are the raw material from which melody and harmony are created.

In fact, musicians have a specific word for the distance between two notes, which is called an *interval*. So, for example, we might say that the interval between B and C is a semitone, or that the interval between A and B is a tone. Just as we were able to give unique names to each of the notes in the major scale, we can also give names to the intervals created between the tonic and each of the other notes in the scale:

The different names may seem arcane, but they all have specific meanings and each corresponds to a certain number of semitones, as shown below the stave. As you can see, we've come across one of these names before: the *octave* is just the name of the interval between the first note of the scale (the tonic) and the last. Each of these intervals has its own characteristic sound, which can be exploited in melodies. Learning the unique sound of each interval is a vital skill for all musicians – with practice, it allows us to hear what music sounds like just by reading the notation. This in turn allows musicians to *sightread* music notation; that is, to play music that we've never seen before directly from the notation.

Interval hint

Note that we could have used any major scale to demonstrate the names of the intervals. This is because the pattern of tones and semitones is the same for all major scales, and therefore the pattern of intervals is also the same

Online material

Visit **www.hybrid publications.com** for a list of famous melodies that use each of these intervals – an ideal way of remembering the unique sound of each one.

Let's do a couple of exercises to reinforce the concept of intervals and to help you remember the interval names. Here are a selection of intervals – this time from the scale of G major – see if you can name them:

If necessary, count up the number of semitones between the two notes and then refer back to the diagram on page 115. Or, just count up from the tonic (G) to figure out which degree of the scale the second note is; this will then give you a strong hint as to the name of the interval!

Now let's do the opposite; here you need to write the relevant intervals onto the stave. To make things more interesting, this time we've chosen intervals from the D major scale, so remember to include any necessary accidentals:

Major 6th   Perfect 4th   Octave   Major 7th

Finally, here's a slightly more tricky exercise. Listen to **Audio track 54** – it contains two intervals, each one played three times. In both cases the first note is C and the intervals come from the C major scale. Try singing up the scale until you reach the second note; then write the relevant note on the stave below, together with the name of the interval:

Don't worry if you don't get this one straight away – it's not easy!

More intervals

Back in Chapter 4, when we talked about accidentals, we mentioned that there were only 12 notes used in all of Western music, corresponding to the 12 keys in one piano octave.

We've seen that certain gaps, or intervals, occur in the major scale between the tonic and the other notes of the scale and we've named these seven intervals. But if there are 12 possible notes, it stands to reason that there must be 12 possible intervals, so where are the missing five? Well, these missing five intervals do occur in the major scale, but not between the tonic and any of the other notes in the scale. Before we track down these elusive intervals, let's map out our 12-note collection and name all 12 intervals:

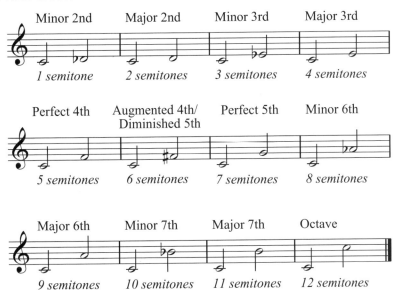

Evil interval?

The interval of the diminished 5th used to be known as *Diabolus in Musica* – "the devil in music" – and was avoided by composers of religious music. Nowadays we're not so superstitious although the interval does crop up repeatedly in heavy metal music.

Notice that one interval has two possible names – it's the note that occurs right in the middle of our collection of 12 notes, exactly halfway between the two tonic notes. Depending on context, this interval can be called either the *diminished fifth*, or the *augmented fourth*. Notice too that most intervals occur in two "flavours", major and minor, with the exception of the octave, the fourth and the fifth. Minor intervals are always smaller than major intervals, as you might expect from their name.

Finding the missing intervals

So the five intervals that don't exist between the tonic of the major scale and the other degrees of the scale are as follows:

Minor 2nd

Minor 3rd

Augmented 4th/diminished 5th

Minor 6th

Minor 7th

It shouldn't come as too much of a surprise that most of these intervals are "minor" intervals. As some of you may know, there is also a minor scale in music and most of these intervals can be found in their "natural habitat" there. However, all these intervals *can* be found in the major scale, as shown below:

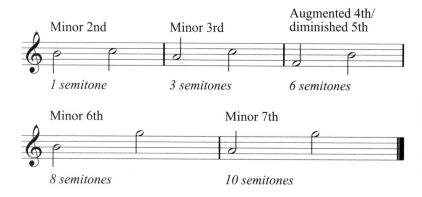

In fact, some of these missing intervals can be found in more than one place. Try finding two minor thirds and two minor seconds in this scale of D major:

Remember, you won't find these intervals based on the tonic, so try measuring intervals from other notes of the scale.

Beyond the octave

So now we can describe every single possible interval that can be found within one octave. But what happens if we have two notes that are more than an octave apart – how would we describe that interval?

Fortunately, it's very simple. Look at the example below; here we have a C on the bottom ledger line of the treble stave with a D over an octave above it:

To get from the middle C up to the D, using intervals we know, we could go up by one octave, and then go up again by a major 2nd. Musicians simplify this, and just add seven to the smaller interval, so we say that the two notes are a major 9th apart. If you count up the number of letter names from middle C to the D shown above, you'll find that there are nine. Here are all the intervals in the second octave:

Notice that each interval appears exactly as the intervals in the first octave, with seven added to it. So a major 3rd becomes a major 10th, a perfect 4th becomes a perfect 11th and so on. Intervals larger than two octaves are relatively rare, so you won't need to worry about naming anything larger than a major 14th.

Jargon buster

Intervals of greater than an octave are known as *compound intervals*. To add an octave to any interval just add 7:

Minor 3rd plus 7 = **Minor 10th**

Major 2nd plus 7 = **Major 9th** and so on...

Worksheet 11 (answers on page 169)

1. Write the names of these intervals from the C major scale under the stave:

2. Write these intervals from the D major scale on the stave. We've given you the starting note in each case:

Major 2nd   *Perfect 4th*   *Major 6th*

3. Try to find the interval of a minor 6th in this scale of G major:

4. Name these compound intervals:

5. What is the alternative name for the interval of a diminished fifth?

6. What was this interval known as in medieval times?

7. How many semitones are equivalent to the following intervals?
a. Minor 3rd
b. Major 3rd
c. Perfect 5th
d. Minor 7th
e. Octave

Answers

Answers to this worksheet can be found on page 169.

Online material

Additional worksheets are available at **www.hybrid publications.com**.

Chapter 12: Compound Time

Back in Chapter 7 we looked at the concept of *meter,* and introduced time signatures as a convenient way of specifying the number of beats in a bar, and which note value we are using to count in. In this chapter, we're going to introduce two new time signatures.

Let's start by reviewing the 3/4 time signature, introduced back in Chapter 7. As you'll recall, the three at the top of the time signature tells us that there are three beats in the bar, while the four at the bottom tells us to count in crotchets. Listen to **Audio track 55** to remind yourself of the feel of 3/4 and count along with this example.

Time tip

Just like a fraction, the top number of a time signature is known as the **numerator** and the bottom number is called the **denominator**.

Audio track 55

Let's imagine that we have another piece, also in three, but that this time we are going to count in quavers rather than in crotchets. So the top number of the time signature remains as three, but we change the bottom number to eight to signify that we are going to count in quavers. Listen to **Audio track 56** to hear what this sounds like:

Audio track 56

Because the quaver is a shorter note value than the crotchet, pieces in 3/8 tend to be faster than pieces in 3/4 (although this doesn't have to be the case). As you count along with **Audio track 56**, note how fast the beats are going by and then try just marking the first beat of each bar, which you may find easier.

Now let's imagine that instead of having three quavers per bar, we double up and include six quavers in each bar, grouped into two sets of three. The time signature needs to have 6 at the top, and 8 at the bottom, telling us that each bar contains six quavers:

Audio track 57

Listen to **Audio track 57** to hear what this sounds like. Again, count along and notice how fast the tempo is – it's actually quite awkward to count six quavers per bar when they are going by this quickly. Instead of counting each quaver, why not try counting each group of three quavers. Start by counting "1-and-a, 2-and-a" and then eventually drop the "and-a" and just count "1, 2".

Threes and twos

The compound time signature of 6/8 has the same total number of beats per bar as 3/4. Both meters contain six quavers per bar, but in 3/4 they are divided into three groups of two and in 6/8 they are divided into two groups of three.

This type of time signature is called a *compound* time signature because it is basically a cross between two beats in a bar (called a *duple* meter) and three beats in a bar (called a *triple* meter). There are two strong beats in the bar, each of which is divided into three sub-beats. This is an important difference because this is the first time that we have divided beats into three. Up to this point all the divisions in the bar have been even numbers: two quavers in a crotchet, two crotchets in a minim etc. Here's another example of a piece in 6/8 time; listen to **Audio track 58** and count along.

Audio track 58

From six to 12

The compound time signature of 6/8 is counted as two in a bar, with each beat subdivided into three. Logically, then, it should be possible to construct other time signatures, with three and four beats in a bar, which are also subdivided into threes instead of twos. Sure enough, we can do that very thing. Let's take an example with three groups of three quavers per bar. We need a time signature of nine quavers per bar, so the top number is 9 and the bottom number is 8:

Beaming tip

Notice how we have beamed the quavers together in groups of three. This shows the divisions of the beat very clearly and makes the music easier to read.

Audio track 59

This example is demonstrated on **Audio track 59**.

If we want to create a four-in-a-bar compound time signature we can do so very easily by increasing the number of quaver sub-beats to 12, giving us a time signature of 12/8:

Add up the dots

In a compound time signature, we use a dotted crotchet to signify one beat; the dot after the crotchet increases its length by 50%, so a crotchet plus a quaver = three quavers. Two beats would be represented as a dotted minim (= six quavers) and so on...

Audio track 60

Again, this example is demonstrated on **Audio track 60**. Count along like this: "1-and-a, 2-and-a, 3-and-a, 4-and-a".

Let's try some exercises to reinforce the concept of compound time signatures. To start with, here's an example in 6/8 with some gaps in it; fill in the gaps with rests so that each bar adds up to six quavers:

Remember that a dotted crotchet = one beat. Now try this similar exercise; this time use groups of three quavers to fill in the gaps:

In this example, tot up the number of beats in each bar and then write the correct time signature at the beginning of the stave:

Finally, beam the quavers in this 12/8 example correctly into groups of three:

The pick-up bar

Sometimes in music we want a melody or piece to start on a beat of the bar other than the first beat. We've seen how we can notate this by using rests; for example, here's a melody in 12/8 that starts on the fourth beat of the bar:

Jargon buster

"Pick-up bar" is a term that tends to be used by pop musicians. Classical musicians call it an "anacrusis", or "upbeat", but it's exactly the same thing

Sometimes musicians call this first bar a pick-up bar, because it's where we "pick up" the melody. It's a very common feature of music of all genres and as we've come to expect musicians have found a way to simplify its notation. Put bluntly, we just miss out the rests at the beginning of the bar and start with the first note, like this:

This is the only instance in music notation where a bar can have fewer beats than is specified in its time signature. (In fact, strictly speaking the last bar of the piece should be shortened by the number of beats in the pick-up bar, so that, overall, the correct number of beats appear.) When you see a piece of music that starts with a pick-up bar, you need to mentally insert the missing rests before you start to play or sing. To start with it is a good idea to actually count the missing rests before you begin, like this:

Worksheet 12 (answers on page 170)

1. Add the appropriate time signature at the beginning of this example:

2. Add the appropriate time signature at the beginning of this example:

Answers

Answers to this worksheet can be found on page 170.

3. Fill in rests to complete this pick-up bar:

4. Fill in the gaps in this piece with rests to ensure that each bar contains nine quavers:

Online material

Additional worksheets are available at **www.hybrid publications.com**.

5. Fill in the gaps in this piece with rests to ensure that each bar contains 12 quavers:

6. What's the alternative name for a pick-up bar?

Chapter 13: Articulation

Right back at the start of this book we described music as "organised sound" and we identified two key characteristics of music as pitch and rhythm. In the previous 12 chapters we've explored these two elements in detail, providing you with the tools to understand how to write down (and read) a huge variety of different pitches, rhythms and meters.

However, there's more to music than just playing the right notes in the right order! Any given pitch and rhythm can be interpreted in different ways by musicians, by changing the manner in which it is played. For example, it could be played quietly or loudly, smoothly or jaggedly, aggressively or calmly, and so on.

These various techniques can be lumped together under the term *articulation*; or to put it another way, articulation describes *how* a note or phrase should be played. In this chapter we're going to look at different ways of notating this information so that it can be read and understood by musicians.

Dynamics

Perhaps the simplest way in which a performer can interpret a given melody or phrase is to vary the volume with which it is played. Musicians call the variation of of volume throughout a piece *dynamics*.

A piece played at the same volume all the way through can become monotonous, so musicians use dynamics to add light and shade and to emphasise elements of pitch, rhythm, structure and harmony.

So, how do we notate different dynamic levels in a piece of music? Well, each *dynamic level* (loud, quite, very loud etc.) has a symbol that is written under the music – the musician simply reads these symbols and plays at the appropriate loudness. For historical reasons, these symbols are actually abbreviations of Italian words. Overleaf, we've given a table of dynamic levels, abbreviations and the original Italian words to which they refer.

Science bit

The loudness of a sound is related to the **amplitude** of the sound wave. We measure loudness in decibels (dB) – 0 dB is the threshold of human hearing, 60 dB is the level of normal conversation, and 110 dB would be the sound level at a rock concert.

Dynamic level	Symbol	Italian term
Very quiet	pp	*pianissimo*
Quiet	p	*piano*
Quite loud	mf	*mezzo-forte*
Loud	f	*forte*
Very loud	ff	*fortissimo*

If we want to create dynamics levels at either extreme, we simply keep adding letters, so *fff* would mean very very loud, while *ppp* means very very quiet.

Dynamics in practice

Dynamic markings of the type described above are the very crudest means that a musician has at his or her disposal, but they can still be highly effective. One simple technique is to juxtapose loud and quiet sections to form an *echo* effect:

In this example the first four bars are played *fortissimo*, while the second four bars are played *pianissimo*. There's no difference in the musical material being played, so the difference in dynamic level adds interest to what could otherwise have been a slightly repetitive phrase.

Listen to **Audio track 61** to hear what this sounds like and then experiment with playing it yourself. Why not try swapping the dynamic levels round and play the first four bars quieter then the second?

> **Hint or tip**
>
> Some early instruments, such as the **harpsichord**, can only play at one dynamic level. The piano (or *pianoforte*, to give it its full name) was so called because of its ability to play both quietly and loudly.

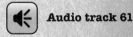

Audio track 61

Changing dynamics gradually

This system of dynamic levels is fine if we want to change suddenly from one level to another, as we did with the echo example on the previous page. While this can produce pleasing effects, it's more common for musicians to want to change the dynamic level gradually; for example, getting gradually louder as the music approaches a climax, or getting gradually quieter as a piece subsides.

There are two simple symbols that we can use to do this, as shown below:

Notice that the piece starts at a dynamic level of *p* (quiet) and ends at a dynamic level of *f* (loud). In between these two symbols are two lines that start at a point and then diverge. This symbols tells the musician to get gradually louder – in Italian the term is *crescendo*. If we want to do the reverse, and get gradually quieter, we simply reverse the symbol:

In this example we start out at *f* (loud) and get gradually quieter, finishing at a dynamic level of *p*. The Italian term for getting gradually quieter is *diminuendo*, or *decrescendo*.

Alternatively we can simply write the relevant Italian terms directly onto the score. They are usually abbreviated as *cresc.* and *dim.* respectively, although you may see them written out in full. Occasionally you may see the phrase *crescendo poco a poco*, which just means *get louder little by little*.

Why Italy?

We'll be coming across a lot of Italian words in this section. Italian is used a lot in music because of its pre-eminence at the time that music notation was being developed. French, German and English are also used, of course, but musicians of all nationalities still use Italian words when describing a performance.

Online material

Visit **www.hybrid publications.com** to download a one-page Quick Guide to musical terms and jargon.

Articulating individual notes

Dynamic levels, crescendos and diminuendos apply to regions or sections of music. However, we also have a variety of options for articulating individual notes, each of which can be notated.

Perhaps the simplest form of articulation that can be applied to a note is an *accent*. This tells the performer that the indicated note should be played more forcefully than the other notes around it and is indicated by a small "wedge" shape, like this: >

Audio track 62

Natural rhythm

Some notes in the bar are naturally more accented than others. The first beat of the bar, for example, often receives more emphasis, and it is the deliberate displacement of this rhythmic accent that we call syncopation.

The accent mark is placed above the notehead that it refers to – listen to **Audio track 62** to hear the effect. Note that the accent effect is a combination of a more aggressive attack at the beginning of the note and increased volume. The accent mark has to be interpreted in the context of the prevailing dynamic level at the time – an accented note in a *pp* section will be quieter than an accented note in an *ff* section, for example. If a stronger accent is required then this symbol is used:

This note would be interpreted with an even stronger attack and dynamic level than the ordinary accent mark. Alternatively, the Italian term *sforzando* can be used to indicate a note or notes that should be played suddenly louder. This is usually abbreviated as *sfz*.

Staccato and marcato

An accent mark tells us to alter the dynamic level of an individual note from that of the others around it. It's also possible to indicate that the rhythmic value of a note should be changed slightly.

Listen to **Audio track 63** and follow the music example below. In particular look out for the small dots above some of the notes:

Audio track 63

Those dots are known as *staccato* marks, and they tell the performer to shorten those notes slightly. (Staccato is another Italian term, literally meaning *detached*.)

In fact an alternative way of writing the above example would be to replace the staccato crotchets with quavers and quaver rests, and the staccato quavers with semiquavers and semiquaver rests.

In contrast to the staccato mark, it is also possible to indicate that certain notes should be emphasised or "leaned" on. This is indicated by a small horizontal line over the notehead, as in bars four and eight of the example below. This type of articulation is known as *marcato*, literally meaning *marked*, and is considered to require less force than an accent.

Top tip

Staccato and marcato marks are usually placed above or below the notehead, on the opposite side to the stem. Sometimes a passage may be marked as *sempre staccato*, which means 'always staccato', and in this case the individual staccato dots are not marked.

Legato

The opposite of *staccato* playing is known as *legato*, yet another Italian term, which literally means *tied* or *linked*. When a passage is marked as legato (or sometimes *sempre legato* – *always* legato) it is an instruction to the player or singer to minimise the gaps between notes so that they flow as smoothly as possible into one another. For a singer or wind player this generally means singing the passage in one breath.

Legato passages can also be indicated by the use of *phrase* marks. These long curved lines indicate musical phrases, and the gaps between them indicate where the music "breathes" – and, in the case of singers and wind players, the gaps indicate literally where breaths can be taken.

In this example, the phrase marks indicate two legato phrases.

It's no coincidence that music uses words like "phrase" which are borrowed from language. Just like spoken English (or any other language for that matter) music falls into natural phrases, and just as in language these phrases are punctuated with rests, pauses and gaps.

The links between language and music are too complex to detail here, but they make for a fascinating area of study. For example, there is some evidence to suggest that we learn musical phrasing and structure as babies before we learn to speak, and that music itself is an even more basic human mental structure than language. In other words, music is a root of language, rather than the other way round.

Tempo

As we've seen in our discussions on meter, the speed at which a piece of music is played – its *tempo* – is vitally important. There are several ways in which musicians and composers have traditionally indicated the speed at which a particular piece should be played. From the 20th century onwards it has been possible to specify tempo in the form of a number of *beats per minute (b.p.m.)*. With a device known as a metronome it is possible to generate a click at any given b.p.m. which then gives the tempo accurately.

In the example below the tempo is specified at the beginning of the piece in the form "crotchet = 120", meaning that the tempo should be set to 120 b.p.m. Note that the unit used for measuring b.p.m. corresponds to the counting unit as specified by the lower number in the time signature. Listen to **Audio track 64** to hear this:

Prior to the 20th century (and to this day in most classical music) speeds were specified by a range of Italian terms that give approximate indications of tempo. A few of the most common are indicated below, together with approximate b.p.m. values:

Italian term	Meaning	Approximate b.p.m.
Vivace	Quick	120-140
Allegro	Lively	100-120
Andante	Walking pace	70-100
Adagio	Slowly	50-70

Speed fact

Computer music sequencers use b.p.m. to specify tempo. When DJs mix two records together they try to match the b.p.m.'s of the two songs exactly so that they blend together.

Audio track 64

Tempo proviso

It should be noted that these are only approximate b.p.m. values and these can vary considerably depending on meter and style.

Jargon buster

Accelerando
Speed up
Rallentando
Slow down
Ritenuto
Slow down
A tempo
Back to the
original speed

Changing tempo gradually

Just as we can specify gradual changes in dynamic level, so we can also specify gradual changes in tempo. A piece of music rarely stays at one tempo for its entire duration; for example it may slow down towards the end, or change speed for a contrasting section.

You can probably take a guess at what the term *accelerando* means – speed up gradually. There is a choice of two Italian terms for the opposite, slowing down gradually; we can use either *rallentando* or *ritenuto*. These three terms are abbreviated as *accel.*, *rall.* and *rit.* respectively.

Here's an example of the use of rall. at the end of a piece (you can hear what this sounds like on **Audio track 65**):

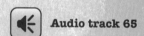

After a tempo change in the middle of a piece, we can reset the tempo to its original value by the use of the term *a tempo*, literally meaning *in time*. In this example, there is a rallentando at the end of bar 4, but the a tempo indication at bar 5 tells us to continue playing at the original speed. Listen to **Audio Track 66** to hear it:

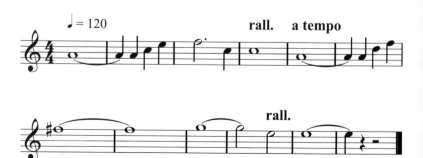

Audio track 65

Audio track 66

Ornamentation

Ornamentation is the term that musicians give to decoration that is applied to a melody – in the same way that a carpenter might apply ornamentation to a plain table leg or cabinet, with the aim of making it more interesting and appealing. Ornamentation is used in all types of music and in all periods, from Bach right through to R'n'B and it always involves the decoration of a basic melody with extra notes, which are often left to the performer's discretion. In music notation we use some specific symbols to indicate to performers that a particular type of ornamentation should be used – it's a form of musical shorthand which saves us from having to write out the ornament in full.

Probably the best known musical ornament is the *trill*. This tells the performer to alternate the pitch that is notated with (usually) the note above it, as fast as possible. There are some fairly complicated rules that are used to decide exactly which two notes should be alternated, but that's beyond the scope of this book. In the meantime, listen to **Audio track 67** and follow the example below:

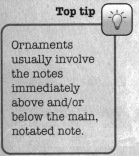

Audio track 67

Look out for the trill symbol in bars 1, 2 and 4 and see if you can spot it on the recording; notice that the note value of the trilled note is still observed. Musicians often vary the speed of the trill, perhaps starting slowly and speeding up towards the end of the note. You can hear trills used in the music of classical composers like J. S. Bach and Mozart, but they're also used in pop and rock music by artists like Jimi Hendrix. On instruments like the harpsichord they allow the player to sustain notes that would otherwise 'die', while for other instrumentalists they provide a simple way of livening up a long note, which might otherwise be slightly uninteresting.

> **Top tip**
>
> Ornaments usually involve the notes immediately above and/or below the main, notated note.

Grace notes

Grace notes are another simple form of ornamentation. They are simply small extra notes that are added to melodies to enhance them and they fall into two main categories: *appoggiaturas* and *acciacaturas*. Don't be put off by these fearsome sounding Italian terms, they're both quite simple to understand and play.

An *appoggiatura* (literally, *leaning note*) is a small extra note that exists outside of the normal system of note values in the bar – that is, it doesn't affect the total number of beats in the bar. It "borrows" a bit of time from the note that follows it, so that the overall beat and meter is not disturbed. Again, there are some fairly complex rules that specify exactly how long an appoggiatura should be in relation to the note that follows it. However, as far as we are concerned we will assume that the grace note takes half the value of the note after it, so that an example that is notated like this, with a grace note appearing in bar 3...

 Audio track 68

... would be played like this, as **Audio track 68** demonstrates.

Note how the crotchet in bar 3 following the appoggiatura has been divided into two quavers. Note too how the performer "leans" on the appoggiatura, releasing the pressure for the main note. In this sense the grace note is more important than the note that it ornaments.

The *acciacatura* looks very similar to the appoggiatura, which, combined with its similar name, can lead to confusion. However, the musical effect of the *acciacatura* is very different.

Unlike the appoggiatura, the acciacatura (literally, *crushed note*) doesn't borrow time from the note that follows it; it is literally crushed in as closely as possible to the note after it, so that it has almost no time value. Here's an example:

Audio track 69

Rock'n'roll!

Crushed notes are a feature of rock'n'roll piano playing, where they mimic the effect of a guitar player bending a guitar string to change its pitch. Players like **Jerry Lee Lewis** and **Little Richard** were influential practitioners.

Note the small line intersecting the stem and flag of the grace note – this is what distinguishes the acciacatura from the appoggiatura. Listen to **Audio track 69** to hear how it sounds.

Finally, here's a longer piece that combines many of the symbols and markings that we've discussed in this chapter. Follow the notation as you listen to **Audio track 70** and try to spot the effect of each piece of articulation and dynamics:

Audio track 70

Articulation, dynamics and phrasing help to bring music alive, and recording them is an essential job of music notation.

Worksheet 13 (answers on page 171)

1. Join up the Italian terms for different dynamic levels with their English counterparts:

forte	quiet
pianissimo	very quiet
mezzo-forte	very loud
piano	quite loud
fortissimo	loud

2. Identify the different articulation and dynamic markings in this example. Each one is marked with a different letter:

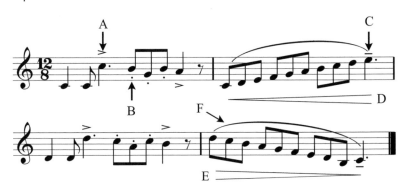

 Answers

Answers to this worksheet can be found on page 171.

 Online material

Additional worksheets are available at **www.hybrid publications.com**.

A:

B:

C:

D:

E:

F:

Chapter 14:
Three Into Two

In Chapter 12 we looked at some time signatures in which each beat is divided into three, rather than two. In this chapter we're going to explore further the tension between threes and twos in rhythmic notation.

As we've remarked before, in time signatures like 2/4, 3/4 and 4/4 the rhythmic structure of music is built up by dividing beats and sub-beats in two. When we first introduced rhythmic notation we started with the semibreve and divided it in two to form the minim, in two again to form the crotchet, and so on to generate quavers and semiquavers.

However, we saw that in time signatures like 6/8 and 12/8 there is another way of dividing rhythmic values. In these cases, the basic beat is a dotted crotchet, which we divide into three to give us quavers. So what would happen if we were to divide a crotchet beat of 4/4 into three? It turns out that this is something that musicians need to do quite a lot, so we've invented a symbol to represent it:

In this bar of 4/4, each beat has been divided into three. The symbol that we use for this looks like three quavers beamed together with a small bracket over the top, split by the number three. This symbol is known as a triplet and it simply means 'play these three notes in the time of two'. In other words, we know that there's only time in a crotchet beat for two quavers, so shorten each note so that we can get three of them in.

A more mathematical way of looking at it would be to say that triplet quavers are each worth a third of a beat, whereas a regular quaver is worth half a beat.

Add it up

All other meters can be built up from sub-groups of 2s and 3s. For example:

5/4 = 3/4 + 2/4
6/4 = 3/4 + 3/4
7/4 = 3/4 + 2/4 + 2/4

Here's an example that mixes regular quavers and triplet quavers:

Audio track 71

Tuplet triplet

Skilled musicians can play tuplets of great complexity in perfect time. It's not uncommon to see rhythms like 13 in the time of 12, or 17 in the time of 16.

Listen to **Audio track 71** to hear what this sounds like. Count along and notice the difference between the regular quavers (counted "1-and, 2-and" and triplet quavers "1-and-a, 2-and-a". In fact, the triplet quaver is just a specific example of a generic concept in music notation called *tuplets*. A tuplet is any group of notes that follows the form: "X number of notes in the time of X". So, for example we could apply the triplet bracket to crotchets, which would translate as "play three crotchets in the time of two":

This is a more complex rhythm than triplet quavers, which fit neatly within crotchet beats; once we move to triplet crotchets the second and third crotchets of each group no longer fall on easy divisions of the beat, because each triplet crotchet is worth 2/3 of a beat.

We can extend the concept even further and have a bar of triplet minims (three minims in the time of two):

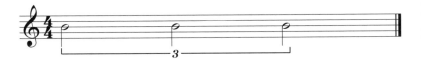

Again, this rhythm cuts across the beats of the bar, with only the first triplet minim falling on one of the main beats.

Taking tuplets further

And why stop at threes? The tuplet format allows us to specify that almost any number of notes can be played in the time of any other number of notes. In modern scores it's not unusual to see tuplets specifying 15 in the time of 14 or other such mind-boggling rhythmic concepts. We're not going to go that far, but we can extend the concept of triplets to quintuplets, which, as their name suggests are five notes played in the time of four:

In this example we have five semiquavers played in the time of four. So instead of each semiquaver being worth 0.25 of a beat (one beat divided by four), each quintuplet semiquaver is actually worth 0.2 of a beat (one beat divided by five). In practice many musicians would think of this rhythm as a triplet semiquaver followed by two regular semiquavers (or vice versa), but you get the general idea.

Here's a final rhythmic brain teaser for you. Try clapping the rhythm below with both hands. The left hand claps triplet quavers and the right hand claps regular quavers.

Triplet tip

If you're having trouble with this exercise, remember that the second quaver should fall exactly in between the second and third triplets.

Listen to **Audio track 72** to hear how it sounds and use your balance to control to fade out each side. It's tricky but very satisfying when you get it right!

Audio track 72

Triplets and compound meters

Eagle-eyed readers may have spotted that there is a link between triplets in time signatures like 4/4 and the compound time signatures that we introduced back in Chapter 12. After all, both allow us to divide the beat into groups of three.

If we were to write out a bar of triplet quavers in 4/4 how would that differ from a bar of quavers written out in 12/8?

> **Top tip**
>
> Triplets in 4/4 could be written as 12/8.
> Triplets in 3/4 could be written as 9/8.
> Triplets in 2/4 could be written as 6/8.

Well, the answer is – not at all. These are both equally valid ways of writing the same rhythm. In practice we would probably favour the 12/8 version, simply because it looks a bit neater without those triplet brackets cluttering the stave up. If we're not going to be using even divisions of the beat then there's no reason not to use 12/8.

As we saw in Chapter 12, another common rhythm in compound time signatures is the crotchet-quaver (or quaver-crotchet) combination, like this:

If we wanted to represent this rhythm in 4/4, how would we do it? We still need to represent a total of three quavers in the time of two, but the first two quavers are joined together to form a crotchet.

One way of doing it would be like this:

However, a more elegant solution would be:

Jazz musicians have come up with a completely different solution to the entire problem. Because the triplet crotchet-quaver combination is so common in jazz, they simply assume that all quaver pairs should be played in this way. These are known as "jazz quavers" or "swung quavers", and would look like this...

Swing

...but are actually played as demonstrated on **Audio track 73**.

The key thing to look out for is the marking "Swing" at the top of the piece, which tells jazz musicians to interpret all quavers in this way. The explanation of swing given above is a greatly simplified one – there is an almost infinite variety of rhythmic variation possible within this broad outline and a jazz musician's particular style of swing is considered to be a vital part of their personal musical signature.

Jazz fact

In jazz parlance the opposite of swung quavers are *straight quavers*. In the US, quavers are known as eighth notes, so this becomes "straight eights".

Audio track 73

Online material

Visit **www.hybrid publications.com** to hear this example of a passage played without swing.

Worksheet 14 (answers on page 172)

1. Use triplets to fill in the gaps in this rhythmic pattern:

2. How would a jazz musician interpret this example? Write it out on the stave underneath in 12/8.

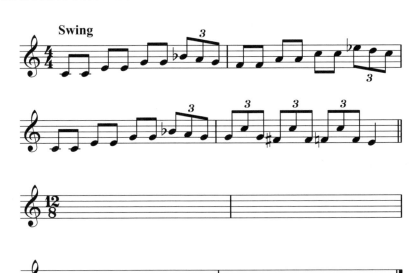

3. Use rests to fill in the gaps in this rhythmic pattern, which includes triplets:

4. A bar of triplet quavers in 3/4 could also be written in which time signature?

Chapter 15: Harmony

Over the last 140 pages we've covered all the basic concepts of music notation, and you can now read and write a huge variety of rhythms and pitches. However, up to this point, we have only ever dealt with melodies – that is to say, single notes sounded one at a time. This is fine if you're a singer, flautist or trumpeter, for example, as you can only physically sing or play one note at a time.

But what about pianists or guitarists whose instruments are capable of playing many notes at once? Or indeed, how would we represent a group of instruments playing together, like a string quartet, or a jazz trio?

When we play single notes one after another we create a melody; when we sound notes simultaneously we create *harmony*, and that's what we're going to be discussing in this chapter.

Triads

As we've already seen there are a bewildering number of possible ways of putting together notes to form melodies – imagine then the huge number of possibilities when it comes to combining notes to form harmony. Fortunately, as with other areas of music, there are some simple rules that will help us to create pleasing and musical combinations.

The basic unit of Western harmony is the triad; as the name suggests a triad consists of three notes:

Here we have a scale of C major, followed by a triad, which we have created by stacking the 1st, 3rd and 5th notes of the scale on top of one another. Listen to the sound of the scale, followed by the triad on **Audio track 74**.

Hint or tip

When we want to notate a group of notes that should be played at the same time, we simply stack them on top of one another vertically. Any note appearing vertically above or below any other note should be played at the same time.

Audio track 74

This triad is known as a triad of C major, because it is based on the root note of the C major scale. We can do exactly the same thing with some of the other scales that we've encountered; here are the triads of G major and D major:

The major triad has some interesting properties. Let's look again at the C major triad, and in particular at the distance between each of the three notes:

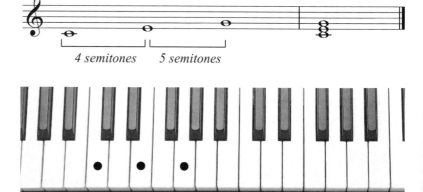

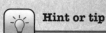

Hint or tip

The interval between the bottom note of a triad and its middle note is vital in creating the unique sound of each triad. It's this major third interval that gives the major triad its particular sound.

The distance between the bottom note, C and the middle note E, is four semitones, or a *major 3rd*. The distance between the bottom note, C, and the top note, G, is seven semitones, or a *perfect 5th*. (Note too, that the distance between the middle note, E and the top note G is therefore three semitones, or a *minor 3rd*.)

This pattern of intervals between the notes of the major triad is the same for every major triad, and gives it its unique sound.

A *triad* is an example of a *chord*; specifically it is a chord with three notes. Not all chords have three notes, however – in fact the word chord is generally used to refer to any number of notes played at the same time. So what can we do with our first chord? Well, we can use it to provide harmony to underpin a melody, like this:

Harmony tip

Any of the notes that are included in the C major triad (C, E and G) will sound good when played over it. However, we can use other notes as well, to create tension and drive the music forward.

Audio track 75

You can hear what this sounds like on **Audio track 75**. Notice that we're now using two staves to represent the music. The treble stave notates the melody while our triads appear on the bass stave. We indicate the notes to be played together by stacking them vertically on top of one another, as in previous examples.

While this example sounds perfectly pleasant it has to be said that it doesn't make for a particularly interesting harmonic backdrop. Fortunately, we can create other triads, which will liven things up a bit. Remember that we created the C major triad by stacking notes 1, 3 and 5 of the C major scale. In other words, we started on C, missed out one note of the scale, added the next one, missed the next one out and added the next one. Suppose we tried this same technique, but instead of starting on the first note of the scale, C, we start on the second note, D. Here's what we would create:

So in this case, we've started on D (note two) and have stacked notes four and six on top of it, to form a new triad. Because we've started on a different note of the scale, this triad contains different intervals:

Bottom note to middle note: 3 semitones (*minor 3rd*)
Middle note to top note: 4 semitones (*major 3rd*)
Bottom note to top note: 7 semitones (*perfect 5th*)

Comparing these intervals to the intervals contained in the major chord we can see straight away that the interval from the bottom note to the top note is the same – a perfect 5th. But the major triad consists of a minor triad stacked on top of a major triad, while this triad consists of a major triad stacked on top of a minor one.

So, this new triad is built on a minor 3rd and it will therefore probably come as no surprise to learn that it is called a *minor triad*. Let's compare the major and minor triads:

	Major triad	Minor triad
Bottom note to middle note:	*Major 3rd*	*Minor 3rd*
Middle note to top note:	*Minor 3rd*	*Major 3rd*
Bottom note to top note:	*Perfect 5th*	*Perfect 5th*

We now have two different triads that we can use to create harmony. Here's an example of a melody supported by harmony using the two chords of C major and D minor

Jargon buster

Because major chords are the most common chord type we usually don't bother to write the word "major" out. So, if a musician refers to the chord of C, he or she is talking about C major.

Let's continue this process and build a triad on the third degree of the C major scale:

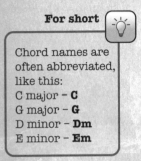

Starting on the note E, we've added the notes G and B to form a new triad. As before, let's look at the intervals contained in this chord:

Bottom note to middle note: 3 semitones (*minor 3rd*)
Middle note to top note: 4 semitones (*major 3rd*)
Bottom note to top note: 7 semitones (*perfect 5th*)

But hang on a minute – this looks very familiar. Aren't these exactly the same intervals we found in our D minor chord?

Yes, they are, which means that this chord must be an E minor chord. In fact, if we continue this process and build triads on every degree of the C major scale, we will find three minor triads: D minor, E minor and A minor:

D minor   E minor   A minor

Not only that but we will also find three major triads: C major, F major and G major:

C major   F major   G major

So, of the seven degrees of the scale, three create major triads, and three create minor triads, which just leaves the last note, B.

If we build a triad on the seventh note of the scale, B, then we end up with a triad containing the notes, B, G and F.

B diminished

Let's look at the intervals contained within this triad:

Bottom note to middle note: 3 semitones (*minor 3rd*)
Middle note to top note: 3 semitones (*minor 3rd*)
Bottom note to top note: 6 semitones (*diminished 5th*)

Triad tip

The bottom note of the triad is known as the *root* note.

There are a couple of interesting properties of this triad; firstly, it consists of two minor 3rd intervals stacked on top of each other. Secondly, this means that the interval from the bottom note to the top note is not a perfect 5th (as with the major and minor triads), but a *diminished 5th* (i.e. six semitones instead of seven). For this reason this chord is known as a *diminished* triad.

The harmonised scale

We can now build triads on each of the degrees of the major scale – this is known as a harmonised scale:

C major
D minor E minor
F major G major
A minor
B diminished
C major

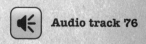
Audio track 76

Note the three major triads, three minor triads and one diminished triad. If we harmonise any major scale we will create this same pattern of major, minor and diminished triads, although, of course, the letter names themselves will vary. Listen to **Audio track 76** to hear what the harmonised scale sounds like; listen carefully to the different chord types and try to hear the differences between them.

Now let's take these seven chords and show how they can be used to harmonise a melody:

Listen to **Audio track 77** to hear what this sounds like.
Note how different chords have been chosen to support different notes of the melody. In particular, look at the last two chords of the piece, G major and C major. This move from a chord built on the fifth degree of the scale to the chord built on the tonic note is very common.

Inversions

So, we've used the major scale to generate three different types of triad and we've seen how they can be used to harmonise a melody. Every time we've shown a triad it has appeared in the same format, exactly as it was when we first generated it. But what would happen if we re-arranged the order of the notes slightly? For example, let's take our C major triad and move the C at the bottom up an octave:

Cadences

The last two chords of a musical phrase are called a *cadence* (from the Latin *cadere*, to fall). The move from G major to C major in this example is known as a *perfect cadence*.

Audio track 77

Online material

Visit **www.hybrid publications.com** to hear examples of other types of cadence.

This new triad contains exactly the same notes as the C major triad, but in a different order, and contains the following intervals:

Bottom note to middle note: 3 semitones (*minor 3rd*)
Middle note to top note: 5 semitones (*perfect 4th*)
Bottom note to top note: 8 semitones (*minor 6th*)

This is quite different to the arrangement of intervals in the major triads that we generated from the major scale, yet this new triad contains exactly the same notes as our first C major triad. Or to put it another way, this new triad shares the notes of the C major triad, but has a slightly different 'flavour'.

When we re-arrange the notes of the triad so that a different note appears at the bottom we call it an *inversion*. In this case, because we've moved the first note of the triad away from the bottom of the triad we call it a *first inversion*. So this chord is known as *C major, first inversion*. Here are the other chords of the harmonised scale in first inversion. In each case, we've simply taken the bottom note of the triad and moved it to the top:

As we've mentioned, first inversion chords have a different flavour to root position chords – they're less stable, and always want to move forward. For this reason they're extremely useful when harmonising a melody as they give the progression of chords a sense of purpose, pushing the music onwards.

When we created our original C major triad, we took the first, third and fifth notes of the scale and stacked them on top of one another. The first inversion of the C major triad that we've just created has the third at the bottom – what would happen if we created a triad with the fifth note at the bottom?

Chord tip

Chords in their original position, as derived from the major scale, are called *root position* chords.

Let's do just that by taking our first inversion chords and moving the bottom note (the third) up to the top, leaving the fifth at the bottom:

These chords are known as *second inversion* triads, and they have an even more unstable feel than first inversion triads. For this reason they're much less common. Here's a harmonised melody using both first and second inversion chords – look out for them as you listen to **Audio track 78**:

Audio track 78

So, to summarise; we can create three different orderings of our different triads – root position, first inversion and second inversion – depending on which note we put at the bottom:

Root position	R, 3, 5	Root at bottom
First inversion	3, R, 5	3rd at bottom
Second inversion	5, R, 3	5th at bottom

The Roman Numeral system

Back on page 150, we said that the pattern of major and minor chords is the same for every harmonised major scale. To prove the point here is the harmonised scale of G major, which shows exactly the same arrangement of major, minor and diminished chords:

As before, you can see that major triads occur on degrees 1, 4 and 5, minor chords occur on degrees 2, 3 and 6 and a diminished triad occurs on the 7th degree. As it turns out, this is quite a useful way for musicians to think about chords because it means that we can specify a chord sequence independently of the key.

For example, we could say that we were going to play the major chord on degree 1, followed by the minor chord on degree 6. This description will work whether we play the chords in C major or G major (or any other major key). In fact, musicians abbreviate this even further and would describe this chord change as '1 to 6'. Because we've already used numbers to refer to degrees of the scale, we use Roman Numerals when referring to chords, so this should be written as 'I to vi'.

In C major this would mean 'C major to A minor', in G major it would mean 'G major to E minor', and so on. When writing chord sequences in this way, we usually write major chords in upper case and minor chords in lower case – here's the complete C major scale with Roman Numeral notation given below the stave:

Note that the diminished chord on the seventh degree is notated as "vii" because it is built on a minor triad.

A common four-chord sequence could be described using this system as "I-vi-ii-V", and this could then be replicated in any key. For example, here is this chord sequence in the keys of G and D major:

Try playing through the two sequences and see if you can spot the similarities. Don't be put off by the fact that the jumps between the chords appear to be different in the two sequences – this is just due to the fact that some chords have been moved up or down an octave to keep them within the stave.

Figured bass

Several hundred years ago, composers and musicians used a different technique to specify harmonic progressions. Known as *figured bass*, the system gave musicians the bass line to play and then told them how to generate the necessary harmony from that bass line. So, for example, if no number appeared below a note in the bass line the musician assumed that he should play a major chord with that as the root note. If a 6 appeared below the note, it told the musician to play another note 6 letter names above that one. This could then be filled out to create a first inversion chord, like this:

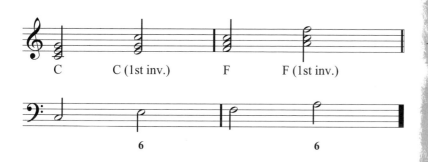

History tip

Figured bass was used during the *Baroque* era of music by composers such as J. S. Bach, Vivaldi and Handel.

Similarly, the figures 6 and 4 below a note told the musician to play notes four and six letter names above the bass note specified – or, in other words, a second inversion. Here's how root position, first inversion and second inversion C major triads would have been written in figured bass:

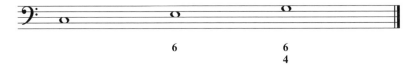

Figured bass was used for hundreds of years to tell harpsichord and organ players which harmonies to play. Although it specifies the overall harmony the specific note choices are left to the individual player and reading (or 'realising') figured bass is a highly skilled technique.

Taking harmonisation further

We've almost run out of space to talk about harmonisation, and we have only scratched the surface of what is a huge subject in music theory. But before we leave the subject we will introduce one further refinement to our system of triads. As you will recall, we took the first, third and fifth notes of the C major scale to create the C major triad, and then repeated this technique for each degree of the scale to create a harmonised C major scale. But why stop at the fifth degree? What's to stop us continuing to stack more notes on top of our basic triads to create even bigger chords? For example, what happens if we add the seventh note of the scale to our C major triad?

By doing this we create a four-note chord containing the notes C, E, G and B. Notice that our finished chord now spans an interval of 11 semitones, or a major 7th, and for this reason this chord is known as C *major 7th*, abbreviated as Cmaj7.

Chord crazy

Any scale can be harmonised, not just the major scale. By harmonising different scales like this we can create hundreds of different chord types, each with their own distinctive sound.

We can apply the same technique to all our other major triads to create a whole family of "7th chords", like this:

So our D minor triad, now has an added C, and spans an interval of 10 semitones, or a minor 7th, and is therefore known as a *D minor 7th*, abbreviated as Dm7. Major and minor 7ths crop up in several places in the scale:

Cmaj7   Dm7   Em7   Fmaj7   G7   Am7   Bm7♭5 Cmaj7

So, we can find major 7th on degrees 1 and 4, and minor 7ths on 2, 3 and 6, as shown above. Let's take a moment to look at the chord on degree 5, where we previously had a major triad. We've now added an F to this chord, so, unlike the other major triads in the scale, this four-note chord only spans ten semitones, not 11. This shape only occurs once when a major scale is harmonised in 7ths and is given a special name: the *dominant 7th* (abbreviated as G7).

The dominant 7th is so named because the fifth degree of the scale is known as the dominant (see page 113), and the dominant 7th chord can *only* be found on this degree of the scale. The dominant 7th chord is particularly important in harmony because it creates a very strong pull back to the tonic chord.

For example, in C major, the progression G7-C (or V7-I in Roman Numerals) is particularly satisfying, and has a strong feeling of finality. This is due to the fact that the chord of G7 contains the interval of an *augmented 4th* (from F to B) which is extremely unstable, and "wants" to *resolve* , with the B moving upwards by a semitone to C and the F moving downwards by a semitone to E.

Resolution

When an unstable chord, such a dominant 7th, moves to a stable chord, we say that it has 'resolved'. This release of tension is what drives the harmony forward.

Let's conclude this chapter on harmony with a complete harmonised melody, including many of the seventh chords that we've just introduced (demonstrated on **Audio track 79**). We've written chord names under the stave, as well as Roman Numeral notation so that you can apply this chord sequence to other keys:

Audio track 79

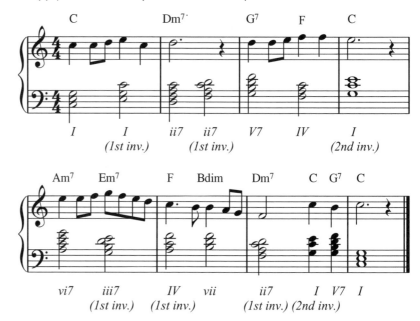

Hint or tip

Look out for the chord change IV–I at the end of bars 3–4. This is another type of cadence, known as the *Plagal*, or *Amen*, cadence.

Even more extensions

Sevenths are known as *extensions* to chords, because they extend the basic triad. It is possible to extend chords even further by adding ninths, elevenths, thirteenths and so on. It's also possible to alter any of the basic chord shapes by raising or lowering certain notes by a semitone, or by adding or omitting certain notes. Using these techniques we can create a huge range of chord types, which allow for great variety when harmonising a melody or composing a piece. These techniques are well beyond the scope of this book, but you can hear them in many musical genres, most commonly in jazz, which pushes harmony to its limit through its use of extensions and alterations. Classical composers such as Richard Strauss, Wagner and Debussy also pushed the boundaries of harmony and are worth a listen if you want to explore harmony further. There's no worksheet for this chapter, but further exercises and information on harmony are available online.

Congratulations

If you've got this far through the book then well done! It was our aim in writing the book to present the concepts of music notation in a simple, easily digestible format that would encourage and reward readers. If you've got right to the end then I guess that means we succeeded!

You've covered a huge amount of information over the previous 160 pages and you should now be comfortable with all the basic concepts of music. Not only that, but you should be able to read and write melody, rhythm and harmony. This will not only allow you to communicate with musicians all over the world in the common language of music, but will give you the tools to record your own musical ideas, learn new pieces of music quickly and with less effort, memorise huge chunks of music and learn more about how music works.

Where now?

The best way to brush up on your reading skills is to play as much music as possible. Only by constantly using your brain to translate musical symbols into real live music will you reinforce what you've learned so far. Remember that music notation is simply a tool to make musicians lives easier – it's not an end in itself. So, use notation to improve your life as a musician and you will find that reading it becomes second nature.

The online resources that accompany this book have been designed in such as way that they can be added to constantly so please continue to check back at **www.hybridpublications.com** for all the latest material.

We've only scratched the surface of many of the subjects covered in this book so there's plenty more to learn. Get out there and find out more about the fascinating and rewarding world of music, but always remember to put what you've learned into practice as a musician. That's what it's really all about.

Worksheet 1 – ANSWERS

1. Write these notes on the stave below (remember that some note names appear in two places on the stave):

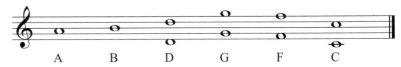

    A   B   D   G   F   C

2. Write the letter names of these notes under the stave:

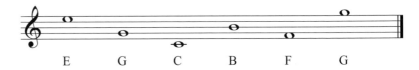

    E   G   C   B   F   G

3. Add notes on the stave to spell these three-letter words:

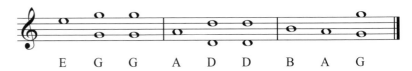

    E   G   G   A   D   D   B   A   G

4. Write down the letter names of these notes underneath the stave to form three more three-letter words:

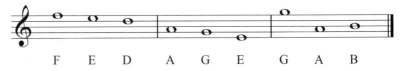

    F   E   D   A   G   E   G   A   B

5. Add a treble clef and time signature to this empty stave, and then add barlines to create two bars. Write a count of 1-2-3-4 under each bar:

    1   2   3   4   1   2   3   4

6. What is the scientific term used to describe pitch?
   A: Frequency

Worksheet 2 – ANSWERS

1. Add one note to each bar to make the total number of beats add up
to four:

2. Add note values to the stave according to the number of beats
written below. We've done the first one for you:

2   1/2 1/2 1   1/2 1/2 1   1   1   4

3. This example contains one bar of unbeamed quavers and
semiquavers. Copy the same rhythm into the second bar, adding beams
as necessary:

4. Use crotchets to spell out these three-letter words, making sure
that the stems point in the correct direction. Where you have a choice
of position for a note on the stave, always choose the higher of the
two:

B   E   G   D   A   D   B   E   E

5. What are the US terms for the following note values?
a. Quaver   **A: Eighth note**
b. Semibreve   **A: Whole note**
c. Crotchet   **A: Quarter note**
d. Semiquaver   **A: Sixteenth note**

Worksheet 3 – ANSWERS

1. Add one rest to each bar to make the total number of beats add up to four:

2. Add rests in the gaps to make the total number of beats in each bar add up to four:

3. Join up the rest values with their equivalent note values:

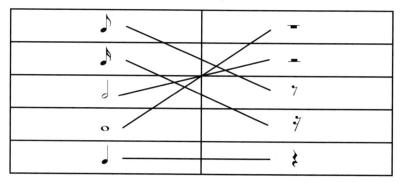

4. Add quaver rests to make up the correct number of beats in each bar:

5. How many semiquaver rests could be fitted into one bar of four beats?

A: 16

Worksheet 4 – ANSWERS

1. Write these notes on the stave below:

C♯   A♭   E♭   F♯   B♭   G♯

2. Next to each note given below write another note that is a semitone higher:

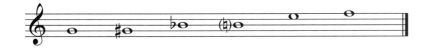

3. Next to each note given below write another note that is a tone higher. Use sharp symbols where necessary:

4. Simplify this example, removing any unnecessary sharps and flats:

5. How would you express these notes using flat signs?

a. C#   **D♭**

b. F#   **G♭**

c. A#   **B♭**

d. G#   **A♭**

e. D#   **E♭**

Worksheet 6 – ANSWERS

1. Simplify this rhythm using dots:

2. Add notes to the stave according to the numbers of beats given below the stave. This will require you to use both dots and ties:

$$3 \qquad 3 \qquad 1^1/_2 \quad 1^1/_2 \qquad 3$$

3. Fill in the missing cells in this table. We've done the first one for you:

1X	𝅝·	=	12X	♪
2X	♩·	=	6x	♪
12X	♪	=	1X	𝅗𝅥·
4X	𝅗𝅥·	=	3X	𝅝
3X	♪	=	1X	♩·

4. Write the number of beats belonging to each note under the stave:

$$1^1/_2 \quad {}^1/_2 \quad 1^1/_2 \quad 2^1/_2 \qquad {}^1/_2{}^1/_2{}^1/_2 \ 1^1/_2 \qquad 3$$

Worksheet 7 – ANSWERS

1. Add the correct time signature to this example:

2. Add the correct time signature to this example:

3. Add the correct time signature to this example:

4. Write out this example again, using a key signature to remove the accidentals:

5. Write out the correct pattern of sharps or flats for these key signatures:

1 flat   *2 sharps*   *3 flats*   *3 sharps*

Worksheet 8 – ANSWERS

1. Simplify this example using repeat marks:

2. Write out this example in full (without the repeat marks):

3. Match up the Italian terms with their correct translation:

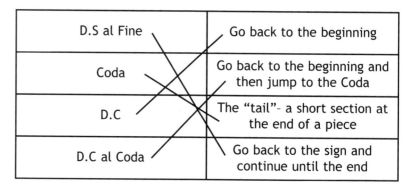

D.S al Fine	Go back to the beginning
Coda	Go back to the beginning and then jump to the Coda
D.C	The "tail"- a short section at the end of a piece
D.C al Coda	Go back to the sign and continue until the end

4. Why is an opening repeat mark not needed at the beginning of a piece?

A: Because you can't go back any further than the start of a piece.

Worksheet 9 – ANSWERS

1. Write these notes on the stave below (remember that some note names appear in two places on the stave):

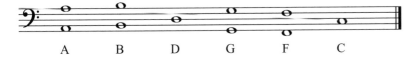

A   B   D   G   F   C

2. Write the letter names of these notes under the stave:

E   G   C   B   F   G

3. Add notes on the stave to spell these three-letter words:

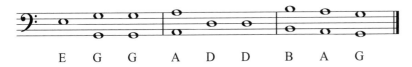

E   G   G   A   D   D   B   A   G

4. Write down the letter names of these notes underneath the stave to form three more three-letter words:

F   E   D   A   G   E   G   A   B

5. Write this example out an octave lower (you'll need to use ledger lines):

Worksheet 10 – ANSWERS

1. Mark the pattern of tones and semitones under this scale of D major:

2. Complete this major scale by using the pattern of tones and semitones to predict what the notes are:

3. Complete this major scale and then deduce the correct key signature:

4. Join up the notes of the scale in the left-hand column with their correct musical names in the right-hand column:

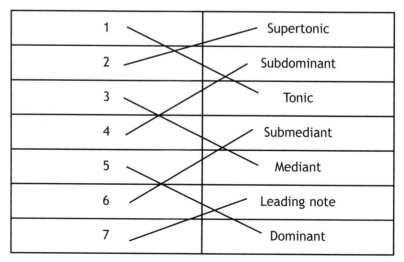

Worksheet 11 – ANSWERS

1. Write the names of these intervals from the C major scale under the stave:

Major 3rd   *Perfect 5th*   *Major 7th*

2. Write these intervals from the D major scale on the stave. We've given you the starting note in each case:

Major 2nd   *Perfect 4th*   *Major 6th*

3. Try to find the interval of a minor 6th in this scale of G major:

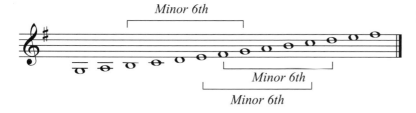

4. Name these compound intervals:

Perfect 11th   *Major 13th*   *Major 14th*

5. What is the alternative name for the interval of a diminished 5th?

A: Augmented 4th

6. What was this interval known as in medieval times?

A: Diabolus in Musica

7. How many semitones are equivalent to the following intervals?

a. Minor 3rd	**3**	d. Minor 7th	**10**
b. Major 3rd	**4**	e. Octave	**12**
c. Perfect 5th	**7**		

Worksheet 12 – ANSWERS

1. Add the appropriate time signature at the beginning of this example:

2. Add the appropriate time signature at the beginning of this example:

3. Fill in rests to complete this pick-up bar:

4. Fill in the gaps in this piece with rests to ensure that each bar contains nine quavers:

5. Fill in the gaps in this piece with rests to ensure that each bar contains 12 quavers:

6. What's the alternative name for a pick-up bar?

A: Anacrusis

Worksheet 13 – ANSWERS

1. Join up the Italian terms for different dynamic levels with their English counterparts:

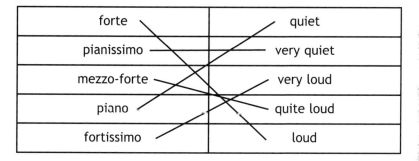

2. Identify the different articulation and dynamic markings in this example. Each one is marked with a different letter:

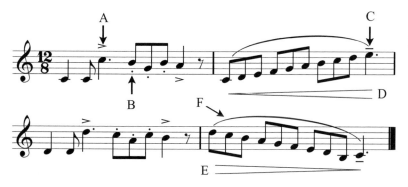

A: Accent

B: Staccato

C: Marcato

D: Crescendo

E: Diminuendo

F: Legato

Worksheet 14 – ANSWERS

1. Use triplets to fill in the gaps in this rhythmic pattern:

2. How would a jazz musician interpret this example? Write it out on the stave underneath in 12/8.

3. Use rests to fill in the gaps in this rhythmic pattern, which includes triplets:

4. A bar of triplet quavers in 3/4 could also be written in which time signature?
A: 9/8

Index

2nd time bars 97
A note 19
accent marks 130
acciacaturas 136-7
accidentals 45-58
    and the bass clef 105
    flats 51-2, 53-5
    and intonation 52
    and key signatures 90-3
    and major scales 112, 113
    naturals 56-7, 69
    one bar rule for 54-5, 56
    remembering 69
    sharps 46-7, 50, 51
    tones and semitones 49
amplitude 127
appoggiaturas 136-7
articulation 127-38
    dynamics 127-9
    individual notes 130
    legato 132
    marcato 131
    ornamentation 135
    staccato 131
    tempo 133-4
augmented 4th interval 117, 118, 119

Bach, J.S. 135, 155
bar lines 23
    dotted 101
    double 101
    final 101
    and ties 75
Baroque music 155
bars 23
    first and second time 97
    five beats in the bar 85
    one bar rule for accidentals 54-5, 56-7
    pick-up 125
bass clef 103-8
    ledger lines 103, 107
    placing notes on the stave 104-6
beamed notes 32, 33, 34, 123
beats
    downbeats 86
    five beats in the bar 85
    and the push 81
    on the stave 23

    and syncopation 77-81
    and tied notes 71-2
    upbeats 87
    see also *time signatures*
Boulez, Pierre 13
boy singers 18
breves 27
Brubeck, Dave 85

C major scale 109-10
    triad 145-6, 147, 148-9, 151-2, 156-7
cadence 151
Cage, John 13
chords 147
    abbreviations for names of 149
    dominant 7th 157
    extensions to 158
    harmonised scales 150-1
    inversion chords 151-3, 155
    Roman Numeral system for 154-5
    seventh chords 156-7
    triads 145-53
chromatic scales 48
clefs
    bass 103-8
    other types of 105
    treble 17-18, 93
Coda 100
compound intervals 119
compound time 121-6
    four in a bar 123
    and pick-up bars 125
    and triplets 142-3
    two in a bar 122-3
computer music language (MIDI) 12
crescendos 129, 130
crotchet rests 40
crotchet-quaver combinations 142-3
crotchets 30-1, 33, 34, 35
    dotted 73, 123
    triplet 140

D major scale 113
    intervals 116, 118
    triad of 146
D minor triad 147-8, 149, 157
dance music 77
D.C. structure 98

D.C./D.S. al Coda structure 100
Debussy, C. 158
decibels 127
denominators 121
diminished 5th interval 117, 118, 119
diminished triads 150, 154
diminuendos 129, 130
dominant 7th chord (G7) 157
dots 73-4, 75-6
    dotted barlines 101
    dotted crotchets 73, 123
    dotted minims 73
    dotted quavers 73
    dotted semibreves 74
    dotted semiquavers 74
    double dotted notes 74
double barlines 101
double dotted notes 74
double octave 119
downbeats 86
D.S. structure 99
duple meters 122
dynamics 127-9

eighth notes 143

F clef see *bass clef*
'Fascinatin' Rhythm' 79
figured bass 155-6
final barlines 101
Fine 99, 101
first time bars 97
five beats in the bar 85
flats 51-2, 53-5
    key signatures 93
    naturals 56, 57
    one bar rule for 54-5
    remembering the flat sign 69
    writing flat signs 53

G clef see *treble clef*
G major scale 111-12
    intervals 116
    triad of 146
Gershwin, George 79
grace notes 136

Handel, G.F. 155
harmony 145-58
    figured bass 155-6
    harmonised scales 150-1, 154

inversion chords 151-3, 155
    triads 145-53
Hendrix, Jimi 135
hip hop 77

intervals 115-19
intonation 52
inversion chords 151-3, 155
Italian terms 129, 133, 134, 136

jazz 77, 80, 158
jazz quavers 143
Joplin, Scott 79

key signatures 90-3, 109
    major scales 112, 113
    naturals 92
    patterns of 93

leading note 113
ledger lines 21, 45, 48
    bass clef 103, 107
legato 132
Lewis, Jerry Lee 137
Little Richard 137

major intervals 115, 117, 119
major scale 109-13, 115
    harmonised 150-1, 156-7
    intervals 115-19
    see also *C major scale; D major scale;*
        G major scale
major triads 145-9, 148, 154
'Maple Leaf Rag' 79
marcato marks 131
mediant note 113
men's voices 14
meter 83, 88, 121
    see also *time signatures*
middle C 21
    12 notes from 48-9, 52
MIDI (Musical Instrument Digital Interface) 12
minim rests 37, 39
minims 28-9, 30, 31, 35
    dotted 73
    ties 75
    triplet 140
minor intervals 117, 118, 119
minor triads 148, 149, 154
mnemonics 29, 68
    for accidentals 69

for note names 29, 68, 105
for note values 59, 68
for rest values 59
Morecambe, Eric 15
Mozart, W. 135
music, defining 13
music notation
how it works 11
origins of 11
reasons for learning to read music 10

naturals 56-7, 69, 92
navigation 95-102
D.C. structure 98
D.C./D.S. al Coda structure 100
double barlines 101
D.S. structure 99
final barlines 101
Fine 99, 101
first and second time bars 97
repeat mark 95-6
Neubaten, Einstürzende 13
note values 26-36
crotchets 30-1, 33, 34, 35
measuring the beats 86-7
minims 28-9, 30, 31, 35
quavers 32-3, 34, 35
remembering 59, 68
and rests 37-44
rhythm workout 60
semibreves 26-7, 29, 30, 35
semiquavers 34-5, 35
summary of 35
notes
A 19
beamed 32, 33, 34, 123
dotted 73-4, 75-6
double dotted 74
names for notes of the scale 113
naming 19
placing on the stave
bass clef 104-6
treble clef 17, 18-21
remembering note names 29, 68
stems 28
tails 32
tied 71-2, 73, 75-6
across the bar 75
see also middle C
numerators 121

octaves 20, 48, 54
intervals 115, 117, 119
and key signatures 91
and the major scale 109
offbeats 77, 81
onbeats 77, 81
organised sound, music as 13-14
ornamentation 135-6

perfect cadence 151
perfect intervals 115, 117, 119
phrase marks 132
pick-up bars 125
pitch 14-16, 25, 45, 127
and intonation 52
patterns 64-5
workout 62-3
see also accidentals
the push 80-1

quaver rests 41
quavers 32-3, 34, 35
and compound time 121-2
crochet-quaver combinations 142-3
dotted 73
tied 72
triplet 139-40, 141, 142
quintuplets 141

repetition in music 95
first and second time bars 97
repeat mark 96-7
rests 37-44
crotchet 40
minim 37, 39
and the pick-up bar 125
quaver 41
remembering rest values 59
rhythm workout 61
semibreve 38, 39
semiquaver 42
and ties 72
rhythm 14-15, 21-2, 25-36, 71-82, 127
displacing 79
dots and ties 71-82
and note values 26-36
patterns 25, 64-5, 79, 81
pulse/beat 22
syncopation 77-81, 130
ties 71-2, 73
workout 60-1, 63

rock'n'roll 77, 137
Roman Numerals for chord sequences 154-5

scales 109-14
    chromatic scales 48
    harmonised 150-1, 154, 156
    and key signatures 93, 109
    see also *major scale*
semibreve rest 38, 39
semibreves 26-7, 29, 30, 35
    dotted 74
    measuring the beat 86-7
semiquaver rests 42
semiquavers 34-5
    dotted 74
    quintuplet 141
semitones 49, 50, 51, 57
    and intervals 115, 116, 118
    and the major scale 110-13
    and triads 146, 148, 149, 150
sharps 46-7, 50, 51
    key signatures 90-2, 93
    and naturals 56, 57
    one-bar rule for 55
    remembering the sharp sign 69
    writing sharp signs 53
sheet music 70
sight-reading music notation 115
singing 13-14, 52
sol fa notation 11
sound levels, measuring 127
staccato marks 131
staves 16-17, 45
    bars and beats 23
    placing notes on
        bass clef 104-6
        treble clef 17, 18-21
    reading 39
    and triads 147
    two stave layout 107
    writing sharps on 47
straight quavers 143
Strauss, Richard 158
subdominant note 113
submediant note 113
supertonic note 113
swung quavers 143
syncopation 77-81, 130
    the push 80-1

tablature 11
tails on notes 32
'Take Five' 85
talking to other musicians 70
tempo 133-4
    gradual change in 134
ties 71-2, 73
    and barlines 75
    dots vs. 75-6
time signatures 23, 83-4, 85-9, 93
    counting in units 85-6
    denominators 121
    different 88-9
    measuring the beat 86-7
    numerators 121
    and tuplets 139-41
    waltz time 84, 88
    see also *compound time*
tones 49
    and the major scale 110-13
tonic note 113
transcription 66-7
treble clef 18, 23, 104
triads 145-53
    and inversion chords 151-3
trills 135
triple meters 122
tuplets 139-41

upbeats 87
US jargon
    eighth notes 143
    half steps 49
    measure 23
    staff 17
    steps 49

Varese, Edgar 13
Vivaldi, A. 155
voices 13-14

Wagner, Richard 158
waltz time 84, 88
women's voices 14
writing your own melody 70